DEAN ANDREA

A Bridge to the Soul:

A Metaphysical Journey

PRINT EDITION

COPYRIGHT ©2019 by DEAN ANDREA

ALL RIGHTS RESERVED

This book is available direct from
the Author (see last pages) or
through online and traditional booksellers,
in print and as an e-book.

A Bridge to the Soul:
A Metaphysical Journey

A Bridge to the Soul: A Metaphysical Journey

Acknowledgments

I would like to thank my wife, Marla, and my children, Sarah and Andrew, for putting up with my quirks and time away from them while I tried to find answers.

I would also like to thank my brothers, Alan and Robert, for again, putting up with someone who was very different and sometimes difficult to understand.

Thanks to Sandy Crowe, Griselda Hale, Kaz Rowley, and Luis Torolla. They have been on a similar path and have been the only non-family friends I have had who have stuck with me through thick and thin -- not an easy undertaking! They all have made it easier for me to stick to this oft-frustrating quest. Also, I send a big hug and lots of love to Connie Pagano. It may sound incredible, but he has cut my hair for the last forty-five years! I give kudos to him not only for being a great hairstylist, but because he has shown me as much genuine love as any friend I have had. It's difficult to explain how someone whom I have not spent much time with outside the barber's chair could have such an influence on me.

If you were to meet him, you would know what I mean.

Also, I want to thank Dr. Norman Shealy, as the time I spent with him at Brindabella will forever be cherished. He is one of the most intelligent, kind, and loving individuals I have had the pleasure of knowing.

I would like to add a special thank you to Tim Kern for his expert help, advice and editing.

Lastly, but certainly not least, I wish to thank my parents Albert and Bernice, who without their unconditional selfless love I would not have made it past my teens.

I would also like to add an apology to anyone I may have hurt throughout my life.
Those of us that experienced extreme hatred directed towards them often lash out at anyone who happens to be in the vicinity.

-ooo-

Preface

There are many paths to freedom.
Even though I reached my breaking point early in life, I have found that it is important to know there is always a way out.
My story is rather unique to say the least. It is my intention to help whoever may read this book, as I believe it does have some relevance to those who have been drawn to explore their inner nature, and to obtain a level of freedom and peace.
Through my life's journey I found that peace that most of us desire.

Contents

Acknowledgments	1
Preface	3
Chapter 1: My Early Years	7
Chapter 2: The Pattern Had Been Set	29
Chapter 3: Beginning My Metaphysical Quest	45
Chapter 4: Future Home	57
Chapter 5: Psychic Unfolding	67
Chapter 6: Past Lives	101
Chapter 7: Bringing In The New Millenium	129
Chapter 8: Sufi Path: the 180-degree Continuum	141
Chapter 9: The End of My Dark Decade of the Soul	155
Chapter 10: Profound Change	167
Part 2: Tips to Find Inner Peace	175
Epilogue	199
About the Author	201
Pre-publication Comments	203
To the Reader	205

Chapter One: Early Years

I was born in Chicago, Illinois in December of 1956. Although my parents were not particularly religious, I was raised Roman Catholic. I attended Catholic schools from kindergarten through my freshman year in college.

From a very early age I experienced past life memories and remembrances of "traveling" during sleep to meet with the angels and masters. I distinctly remember feeling frustrated upon awakening. I truly did not want to be here in the physical. I retained a deep knowing that I went through some sort of process to make me forget specific details of my travels "for my own good."

During my childhood I also had a deep reverence for Jesus, the apostles, Mary, and Joseph. For whatever reason, I felt that Joseph never received the recognition that was due him.

From my earliest memories I seemed to not quite fit in. I was perplexed by the things most people thought important. I also remember having physical pain and fatigue even at this early age. I was admitted into the hospital on more than one occasion to try and get to the bottom of it. Looking back, I now know that I made a soul contract and was on an assignment to experience a lot of physical, mental and emotional negativity.

I will talk about negativity throughout the book. Let me explain that what I term as negative is merely the personality's labeling of it. This is a key point in one's understanding of the Infinite!

I remember well my first day of kindergarten. It was a hot night before that first day, as my brothers and I slept on a mattress brought into our family room. Our childhood home had two window air conditioning units. On hot nights we would sleep in our family room, since it had one of the units, was a relatively large room, and we could close the double doors to help keep the cool inside.

When I woke up that morning, my mom told me I needed to get dressed as it was the first morning of school. I was somewhat afraid upon leaving the safeness of my mom and home.

As I remember, that first day was okay until it was time to go home. The kids were supposed to have a note pinned to their shirts when they arrived at school to let the teachers know how they would get home. They would either be picked up by their parents or guardians, or take a bus. If we were to take a bus, we were to have our bus number written on the note as I believe there were four or five buses.

I was reprimanded for not having my note. I was accused of losing it. The fact was, my mom overlooked this instruction and had never given me one. There was a lot of commotion as the teachers didn't know what to do. I was only five years old and didn't know our phone number, and I assume they didn't have it readily available.

I became frightened as the grownups appeared agitated, and to a small child they appeared frightened as well. They said "Well, we will let all the buses leave and hope your mother will come and pick you up. Now we will have to wait for you!"

We must have waited quite a while, because a couple of the bus drivers came back to school after dropping their kids back home. One of the teachers said, "It's getting late and we will have this bus driver drive you around so maybe you can recognize where you live." I didn't have a clue. Even at five years old I knew that much!

I was really afraid now. As I followed the bus driver to the bus, my mom showed up and told me that she didn't know how I didn't know which bus I should have gone on. (She thought she had told me, but she hadn't.)

To a small child trauma like this can have a lasting effect -- and it did. I was deathly afraid of "missing my bus" for years, even though it made no logical sense as I grew older.

June second, 1962, was a precursor of many of my difficulties in life. On this day, I attended a birthday party for a kid who was in my kindergarten class, which had just ended. It was a much-anticipated event by most in my class. I didn't really know the child who gave the party as my class was pretty large; everyone in the class was invited.

It took place in Harms Woods, a forest preserve near the school we attended. I was the first child in a long procession into the woods to our campsite.

It turns out that I would be first in a long line of events as my last name started with A.

As I recall, there were one or two grownups ahead of me. The grownups reached a fallen log which traversed a stream. I remember hearing them say that it would "probably be okay to let the kids cross over on the log."

Keep in mind, I was just shy of being five and a half years old. Also, since I have severely flat feet I was never able to wear anything but lace-up shoes. (I don't believe I ever wore sneakers or tennis shoes like most kids, as my mom always had me wear leather-soled oxfords.)

The grownups crossed just ahead of me. I had never been hiking or in the woods at this point in my young life. I was afraid and didn't know how deep the stream was. Also, I had never learned to swim and was not familiar with water, other than in a bathtub.

My fear got the better of me, and between that, my shoes, and a spot of bark that let go, I fell in the stream, sort of straddling the log. Both feet went into the water, which it turns out was only two or three feet deep. One of my shoes stuck in the mud as I tried to get out. Both of my feet were soaked with cold slimy water and mud.

Eventually one of the grownups retrieved me and my shoe. After my accident, the grownups asked if each kid wanted to be carried across or wanted to try to cross on their own. From that point on I took a lot of abuse from the other kids, even the ones who were carried across. Kids would constantly bring this up to me.

I was not to live this episode down for many years. In fact, in seventh or eighth grade (seven or eight years later!) a kid came up to me and belittled me about this event which I had long since suppressed.

While I was writing this book, my wife handed me a picture dated 6-2-1962 with the child's name who hosted the birthday party, and that it was taken at his birthday party. It brought back a flood of emotions and long suppressed memories. I had not seen this photo in approximately fifty years and didn't remember it even existed. This is another in a long line of synchronicities I have had since birth.

Once I started elementary school, I soon found that I was not one of the popular kids. I distinctly remember asking myself why this was so. I have vivid memories of wondering why I was perpetually among the last to be picked for Red Rover.

By third grade things really began to change. Between third grade and seventh I put on enough weight to be called fat. From what I now know, energetically, the weight around the middle was a subconscious protection measure to insulate my center of self-worth from abuse. I will go into more detail about this later.

A Bridge to the Soul

This "not fitting in" or "not being popular" turned to my being bullied, ridiculed, and shunned. I could go into long stories about this abuse, and how pervasive and organized it was, but I will just share a few incidents that have often come up when I have done self-healings.

Keep in mind that every day at school was filled with terror for me. There was no respite. This will give the reader a sense of what beliefs were formed in my consciousness. This is a key point in my development and future spiritual searching.

In first grade, I had a nun who did not like me (or anyone else, for that matter). She used to lift me up by my head, literally off the ground. I was only five to six years old! She would also pull my ear so hard that I would go home with an earache.

I had never had ear infections until this time. They became so frequent that I was on a continuous stream of antibiotics. Back then, doctors prescribed antibiotics like water.

My mother wrote a note for me to give to the teacher. It basically said: "Please don't pull my child's ear as he is continually getting ear infections. This is not good for him!"

Well, when I gave my teacher the note, all hell broke loose. She called another nun into the room and said, "Do you know what this child gave me?" My teacher asked me to repeat the contents of the note.

I said, "My mother asks that Sister not pull my ear any more."

My teacher said, "What else did it say?" I was so flustered that I said that was what the entire note said. The nun proceeded to hit me and said: "WHAT ELSE DID IT SAY?"

I was truly terrified by this time and froze. The teacher told the other nun that "His mother is saying that by my pulling his ear he is getting ear infections! Did you ever hear something so stupid?"

As you can imagine, sister did not stop the behavior. It continued that whole first year, as did my frequent ear infections. Also, these reprimands were given to me in front of my classmates, compounding the negativity. The ear infections stopped after that year, although I have suffered from extreme allergies from early childhood on (including chronically plugged ears).

In sixth grade, I had two teachers who were oppressive. They not only knew the bullying that was going on, they supported it. One, a Mr. P., was a mid-twenties single man that had a nervous twitch. It always seemed that his collars were too tight because of this twitch. He would insult me in English class and in Phy Ed. I had him for two years. Whenever I would do pushups, he would yell out, "Andrea, I can hear your stomach hit the floor!"

Once in English class, we had a spelling test. We exchanged papers with the person sitting behind us so that this person would correct the test and grade it. Since I was last in the row, I had to exchange with the first person in the row. When we got our papers back, I had a very low mark. Most of the answers were marked as incorrect.

I raised my hand and a belligerent Mr. P. started to make fun of me for complaining. I started to cry, and that got the whole class going. I explained that you could clearly see that the person who "corrected" my paper used a different color ink, misspelled the words on purpose, and marked them incorrect. Mr. P. just laughed along with my classmates, and made some snide comment directed at me personally.

By the time I was in seventh grade, the chronic hazing had taken its toll. I had become an introvert and was in a lot of physical pain and mental anguish which I now know were the beginnings of a lifelong battle with fibromyalgia, CFS, and PTSD.

From an early age, I had a developed sense of humor which was now largely kept hidden as I didn't want to attract attention to myself. I stopped raising my hand in class; every time I did, it left me open to attack. I became anti-social and frightened and distrustful of most people. I had told my parents about the goings-on and although they loved me, they basically said I needed to fight back. This was foreign to my nature.

Plus, my classmates were so organized and had the complicit support of several teachers. It made fighting a bad decision, or so I thought.

Another example of the hazing that was taking place was again in English class, in seventh grade. We were given an assignment to write a fictional story. I decided to go out on a limb and use my humor. While I was mostly too afraid to show humor, I still had it.

I wrote a story based in Colonial America. I spent a lot of time crafting it and was convinced it was a gem. (It should be noted that even though I was going through all of the abuse, I was an A student with a measured IQ in the genius range. I also started school a year early, as I was born in December. I believe being younger than most of the kids in my grade had a detrimental effect on me.)

I finished what I thought was a masterpiece. To make sure that it was good, I recited it to my older brother. He was in high school by this time. He laughed his socks off. He said, "If you don't get an A on this and if the class and teacher doesn't get hysterical when he hears this, something is definitely wrong."

Each member of the class was required to read his essay out loud in front of the class. *I'm in luck. Mr. P. is out sick and we have a substitute!* I thought I would be safe; I knew Mr. P. would make some snide comment, but now he couldn't!

While waiting to read my story a wave of dread came over me, but I was strong and knew I had a gem. *My turn*. I bravely read the story with as much enthusiasm as I did when I read it for my brother. At the first funny bit, two girls right in the front row started to laugh like crazy. The substitute did, too.

Almost immediately, a couple of the leaders of the "in clique" loudly made some sounds like clearing their throats. I saw everyone in the class turn around and look at them. They gave the "cut it" sign, drawing their palms across their throats.

For the rest of the story, which became even funnier, the only person to laugh was the sub, who seemed perplexed at the class's behavior. Any sign of "supporting" whatever I did was met with retribution from the abusers. The hazing was so complete by now that I was left in an isolated desert of despair.

Another teacher I had in sixth and seventh grade was the worst of all. Ms. G. was her name. She was a very small woman from Iraq, and she looked like Satan himself. I had her for homeroom and French. She immediately fell in with the popular kids and took an immediate dislike of me.

From the beginning of sixth grade through seventh, she made my life a living hell. It was during these years that I started to have thoughts of suicide. From the beginning of sixth grade through the end of seventh she purposefully called me by the name of Dennis. Just to clarify, my name is, was, and always has been *Dean*. No one else in my sixty-one years has called me Dennis. If you remember the old TV show, *Bewitched*, Endora used to call Darrin, Dirwood, or some other goofy name as a way to demean him. This is much the same thing and I believe she came up with the idea from watching the show.

Once, she graded an assignment of mine and called me up to the front of the room. She wrote on the paper, "RUBBISH" and gave it 0%. She said, as I was standing up in front of the class, "The only thing that I can do to Dennis for trash like this is to do this:" Then she had me stand in the front corner of the room, turn so my back faced the class, and fastened the paper to the back of my shirt. I had to stand there for the whole afternoon. Of course everyone in the class had a field day.

Another instance of abuse was when my mom was a chaperone at a school field trip. At one point in the trip, at the Field Museum in Chicago, my mom asked Ms. G. if she had time to make a bathroom stop. Ms. G. said, "Sure, we'll wait for you."

Well, Mom went in and Ms. G. took the class away, leaving me alone, waiting for my mom. Of course, Mom didn't know where they had gone, and it took her quite a while to track the group down. The next day in class, while Ms G. went out of the room, the kids started taunting me saying, "Dennis's mom got lost at the museum and couldn't find her way back!"

I started to protest, as this was one of the first times I found my abusers attacking my family. Ms. G. came back in the room and asked what all the commotion was about. I spoke up and told her what had transpired. She said with a snide smile, "Well, she did get lost." I just started to cry.

During these elementary school years, there were more incidents than I could possibly relate.

Also, while I feel the systematic emotional and mental abuse was the worst, there was also a lot of physical abuse. I was physically assaulted many times:

I had my nose broken in seventh grade for nothing. I was outside at recess. As usual, I was not participating in any activity. I remember standing by a fence. Some of the kids in my class were playing soccer. Someone kicked the ball and it got away from them. It came towards me and I, trying to be nice, kicked it back into the field. The boy who had been chasing the ball down became angry and made some nasty comment to me. I turned away and before you knew it, while I was not even looking at this kid, he hit me in my nose.

I was shocked. The blood was everywhere and I was afraid, in pain, and stunned. I ran to the nurse's office and they called my mom. It turns out I had a fractured nose. Nothing was ever done to the kid who did it, either. This same kid kicked me in the crotch while I was on the ground fighting another boy several months later. I nearly passed out and was sore for over a week.

I was literally in fear for my life every day. I was afraid to go to the bathroom and often had to "hold it" until I got home. If I did go to the bathroom, there would invariably be one of my abusers there waiting for me. They would often try to grab me by the testicles and squeeze. Not a pleasant experience!

As far back as first grade I used to cry before school and tell my parents I didn't want to go. School to me was a stacked deck. It was a battle with too many enemies and no allies.

That first-grade nun was insightful in many ways, but she used her insightfulness in nasty ways. Once, early one morning, she saw that I had been crying. (I had stopped crying long before I had gotten to school.) She accosted me as I entered her classroom and said, "Why have you been crying?" I replied I didn't know, and she told me I was a liar. She knew why I had been crying: *because I didn't want to go to school*. Then she hit me.

Many people have asked why no one ever helped me, or why I didn't more clearly convey what was happening to me. After years of introspection and therapy I am not sure even that I fully know the reasons. I guess I had become so afraid that I sought anonymity. Also, I felt ashamed of not being able to fight back.

I remember feeling paralyzed as I was truly dismayed at people's nastiness. This anger and retribution towards innocent people totally perplexed me. I felt guilty that somehow this must be my doing, etc. As I will explain later in this book, much of this trauma has led me to be a healer and counselor.

There are two other incidents that were difficult for me and stand out: The first one involved playing sports for Mr. P., my phys ed teacher and nemesis.

When we played softball, usually we would get three pitches to hit. I noticed that whoever pitched to me would throw balls that were impossible to hit. I used to complain; everyone would just laugh at me, including Mr. P.

One day I was in the field. They would make me play far in the outfield where no one was likely to hit the ball. On one memorable day, a guy hit a really long fly right to me. Keep in mind, away from the school environment I used to play softball a lot with my older brother and kids in my neighborhood who didn't attend my school. (I used to be okay at it, too.)

So the ball came to me and I caught it. Everyone berated me and said it was "pure luck" that I caught it. They cried, "He just closed his eyes and raised his hands. Somehow the ball just went into his hands!" This was expected, but I wasn't ready for one kid who was never really mean (although certainly not supportive of me) came up and said, "Dean, you have to admit that was pure luck." This really hurt me and stuck with me for years. It seemed as if I couldn't win.

The other incident involved my former sixth grade history teacher. His name was Mr. M. and I was his top student. He seemed to like me and while we were never close, I never remember his disrespecting me until seventh and eighth grade.

By this time, I didn't have him for regular classes any more. He was the football coach, which was a big deal in those grades. Obviously, I would never have gone out for anything as I knew what my chances would be and how I would be treated.

I remember on several occasions he would purposely ignore me; he would never let me join in when he would hit fly balls at lunch time to the kids on the team. His attitude towards me had changed completely. I can only surmise it was because I was not on any of the teams, and he became influenced by the disrespect everyone else was showing me. I felt totally betrayed.

I should note that I did have a teacher in fifth grade homeroom named Ms. Rupee. She has long since passed on, however I want to give her lots of love and thanks as she was the only teacher I have ever had who showed me such love. She did NOT like the main abusers in my class and I was her favorite. This greatly upset the "in crowd." They didn't know how to abuse me when she was around because she was on to them and totally supported me. I don't know much about her, but she must have had great insight. I never got to thank her in this physical existence for the difference she made to me. I often thought of her kindness in those troubled years. I still send her love often.

In eighth grade we had to take dance lessons. This was another place where I was completely torn down, this time mainly by girls. Every class would be a heartbreak for me, being ridiculed and told to my face how ugly, undesirable, and nasty I was.

I remember one instance when one of the girls was told she had to dance with me. She said right in front of me, "Hey everyone, look what I have to dance with!" Everyone began to laugh. I would remain the outcast with no one to dance with, unless the teacher picked partners. The teacher did nothing to try to help me out, either, and he, like the other teachers, saw what was going on.

Once, again in eighth grade, I was in class when one of the popular girls in our grade moved her desk right up against mine. This was in the middle of class and the teacher was teaching. This teacher, whose name was Ms. Adamson, was blackballed by the students, much as I had been.

One day towards the end of the school year Ms. Adamson came into our class and confronted it. She was crying hysterically and told our class how mean we were and how she had really anticipated with joy her new role as teacher (This was her first year at it—what a place to start!).

She spelled out to us how miserable, mean, and horrible our class was to her. There was organized hazing of her just like they had done to me. She said she was considering not teaching any more. I never learned what happened to her.

Back to the story: so this "in crowd" girl moved her desk next to mine and started hugging and kissing me, telling me how great I was. Everyone in the class started to laugh at me, as they all knew what she was doing. She was torturing me like a kid pulling the wings off of flies.

The teacher didn't know what was going on and she got mad at me, which really fueled the laughter at my expense. I felt badly that the teacher thought I was at fault and wanted to explain, but I knew I couldn't.

This girl continued this behavior for the next week, giving me no end of grief. Ms. Adamson had long since lost control of the class and didn't stop the girl's behavior. Like me, she had given up trying.

In eighth grade, my homeroom teacher read us a paper that a scholar had written. It was a study he had performed revolving around great saints throughout history. He had distilled ten outstanding qualities that each of these saints possessed.

My teacher said that our class "…probably wouldn't possess any of these qualities ourselves, as most people don't. So class, don't feel badly if you don't possess any of these qualities."

The author had said that if one would possess just four or five of these that they would probably be very great men or women. When she read them, one by one, from first to last, I was shocked to honestly say to myself, "This is me." Needless to say, I wouldn't have dared to make this known, but it reinforced my belief that I was different.

I believe that as a result of these childhood experiences, and chronic antibiotic use well in to my twenties, I developed what I later came to know as fibromyalgia, chronic fatigue, and PTSD. While these maladies have been a challenge, they have also brought me great insight. They have led me to a place of knowing that whatever may happen in this life, it is for your highest good. I will explain in much greater detail how I came to this conclusion.

Chapter 2:
The Pattern Had Been Set

The summer of 1970 was a strange time for me. I decided to go to summer school and take a pre-algebra course, recommended to help me get a leg up on high school math. This was a difficult decision for me as I absolutely hated school and felt vulnerable there.

During this summer something magical happened to me. From day one in this class, which was held at what would be my new high school, I was not only liked, but admired by everyone in the class.

The teacher, a Mr. Bowen, was the best school teacher I have ever had. He had a way of teaching math that was out of the traditional teaching paradigm. I excelled in high school math and to this day I use some of the tricks he taught us to solve problems.

I was the top student in the class along with one girl who was not only cute but seemed to like me as well. Also, another girl really liked me and appeared to have a crush on me. Kids admired me for my intelligence, made no unreasonable demands on me, and expressed their admiration for me!

I didn't know how to react to this and it would take decades for me to actually trust that people who liked me had no ulterior motives. I would suspect people of making fun of me behind my back. I had become socially awkward and felt extremely afraid when with others. Hence I have had few friends in this life. At this point in my life, I felt I needed to ensure I would never again be a victim.

The second nice event during this summer was that I received a short wave radio. I would spend years enjoying this toy and found "DXing" extremely fun. DXing is looking for distant radio stations all over the world.

I sent away for many QSL cards from Ukraine, Russia, Ceylon, Austria, Holland, Equador, Australia, and many more.

You got QSL cards when you listened to a radio show from various countries. Then you send a letter to the radio station, mentioning which show you listened to, giving details about show content and what type of signal the station had at that time.

One would use a prearranged grading scale called SINPO. S would be signal strength, I is interference, N is noise, P is propagation disturbance (drift), and O is the overall grade. These were all based on a scale of one to five. The cards usually had beautiful scenes from that particular country, much like a neat postcard. DXing gave a lonely boy years of pleasure.

As I wrote this book it occurred to me to have my astrological chart checked for this period of time since such a major shift had occurred. This magic time of acceptance, happiness, attractiveness,and success was extremely short and never occurred again until, through much inner work, I have now embodied the qualities/attractions that I experienced then.

Through much synchronicity I contacted someone who I had heard many times over Chicago radio and had sessions some twenty years earlier. His name is Thomas Pecora, and upon reconnecting with him we both realized how in synch we both are with each other.

He gave me a superb reading about that time and many things currently happening in my life. He told me that at that moment I had five (or more) things in my chart that truly made it a once in a lifetime occurrence. As I intuited, this period was what I will call an initiation into a new paradigm.

There was much more in that reading with Thomas that I won't elaborate on at this time. As you will see, as this magic summer ended, things did get better, as far as abuse was conerned.

I managed to survive elementary school, although I was now severely wounded.

The energy of the summer started to fade. The first day of high school was met with great anticipation, although that first day I definitely experienced a dramatic change in my *modus operandi*. I decided to become a tough guy.

I literally could still feel the "energetic shift" that happened that day. I had started out life as a gentle, humorous, artistic and intelligent child and by age thirteen, I had become driven by hate.

Hate made me feel empowered. Not hate of everyone, but hatred of those whom I labeled the abusers. I became a champion of the downtrodden. I have always been attracted to the more-unpopular people. I see and/or sense something wonderful in them.

By the start of eighth grade, I had become extraordinarily slim and swore to never be fat again. I embarked on a path of physical fitness. I thought of myself as the "Spruce Goose." (This is a reference to the late Howard Hughes' airplane. He designed it as the largest military transport in the world. It was a colossal boondoggle, but he instructed his people to keep it ready if needed. He spent countless millions over the years keeping it ready to join any potential fight.) I now thought of my body as always ready for the onslaught that I knew would come. I felt keeping fit was a matter of survival, literally!

At orientation day, freshman year, I met a kind of dorky-looking guy. Back then I didn't know why I was attracted by his energy, but I was. I knew that the jocks and popular kids were creeps, so I decided to be the protector of the geeks.

At assembly, we sat next to each other. There was a big kid throwing things at my dorky friend. I stepped in and agreed to meet this big kid after school. Although I was afraid, and he was a lot bigger than me, I showed up at the appointed time. This kid brought four of his friends with him. I decided I better throw the first punch. I did and I missed.

I could see that this frightened the big kid and he then asked his friends to gang up on me. This was par for the course for me as I knew from my grade school days how cowardly the bullies were when they were by themselves.

His friends refused, but he kept trying to persuade them. I then told him I wasn't going to fight all of them and left. Although I wasn't totally happy with my performance, I did feel I had turned the corner on my accepting abuse without protest. The animosity between me and this creep went on all through high school. We would often meet in the hallways and I could count on some pushing or some snide comments made. Also, his best friend was my locker mate which fueled a lot of tension. I think my locker mate was afraid of me, as he was one of the kids whom the bully tried to get to help him beat me up.

In high school I did have some friends despite being generally socially dysfunctional. I was a good actor, however. I was more afraid of being
labeled a creep by showing my dysfunctionality, so I managed to hide it pretty well. I didn't understand how to relate to my peers. Looking back, I really didn't trust anyone any more.

Another incident in my freshman year was reminiscent of my falling into the stream in kindergarten. At home, I had been a decent basketball player, especially good at dribbling close by the basket. I had developed this skill and my softball skill away from the school environment. At home, although not popular with the neighborhood kids, I was at least accepted on my own merits.

At school one day, I was shooting some baskets at lunchtime and a coach asked me if I would play with them as they needed another player. I was honored to be asked, as this never would have happened in grade school.

As we began playing, fear took a solid hold of me. I realized how much pressure I was under and how much I must have been putting myself under for years. I would be mortified if I didn't perform flawlessly. Every time one of the coaches passed me the ball, I couldn't even hold on to it. This was not normal for me.

After I dropped three of four passes, they avoided me like the plague. I realized how crippling fear could be. I was devastated that "the only chance I had ever been given" was blown.

About freshman year, I began to golf. In sophomore year I won the fall junior varsity championship at school. As stated earlier, I began to have some painful physical symptoms. This definitely affected my golf, as I practiced chronically. I became a perfectionist as a result of my childhood experience. I wanted, in no way, to let anyone have any way to criticize me or laugh at me.

Golf was an escape for me and I was a prodigy at it. The summer of 1973 was a banner year for me in terms of what I accomplished in hitting a golf ball. I could hit the ball 300 yards at a time when the longest tour player averaged 270.

I was also not fully physically developed. I weighed 130 pounds and my golf was erratic, but still my scoring in no way reflected how I could hit the ball.

Junior year started with great expectation, though by this time I was in a lot of pain. It was really affecting my swing.

My club head speed was measured at 120 mph. Many people at that time told me this was impossible, that even the best tour players couldn't match that. But the speed was verified with was what was then thought of as a precision instrument.

This great club head speed and my constant practicing had an effect on my physical body. The pain became so severe that I was having difficulty holding a jug of milk. I decided to see a top orthopedic surgeon in the Chicago area. He said that the growth spaces in my arms were being pulled apart by my constant practicing. He said I needed to quit hitting balls until the spaces grew
together. If I didn't stop, I would need surgery to put metal pins in my arms to hold them together. This diagnosis was in late summer of 1973.

To make a long story short, I didn't resume hitting golf balls until what would be my junior year in college. At that time, I still had lots of arm pain, however x-rays showed the growth spaces had grown together and I was no longer in danger of separating the bones in my arms. Also, by then, I was starting to experience severe searing fibromyalgia pain.

During my freshman year in college I was going to a small school in central Florida. My dad, who was an excellent golfer, and who started me in golf, was a friend of a touring pro who started a resort north of Tampa. This is one of the main reasons I chose this particular school and location. I had the hopes of really starting to get a "normal" life in college. High school had been better than grade school, by far, so I thought college would continue this upward trend.

I was in for a rude awakening. Golf, at which I excelled until my physical problems, was to be my out. I fantasized how I would become rich and famous. I would then use this fame to get back at all the people who had abused me. I used to daydream of how a certain abuser would come up to me when I became famous and I would act like I didn't remember who he was. I would tell him, "You know, because of my fame, I get all kinds of people coming up to me telling me they used to be my friends. I don't know you from Adam!"

Now golf was on the back burner, I had no friends, I was extremely depressed, and I had the stress of college which I needed to be perfect in. My freshman grade point average was 3.91. I received all As except for two B+, those from the same teacher who, when I complained about the grades, said she didn't believe in giving out As as no one warranted an A, because no one was perfect! This was a big disappointment to me.

And my roommate was a psychopath. He was a bully, and his best friend, who was in our room continually, was a linebacker on the football team. He was huge and, like my roommate, didn't like me because I was a good student.

They were frequently drunk and destroyed many of my things, and we almost came to blows several times.

Every night was torture as I would be nagged by them. I was getting little sleep because of this and was frequently sick with flu-like symptoms. By the grace of God I managed to survive and pleaded with the RA to get me transferred to another room. It took until second semester, but I managed the transfer.

It should be noted here, that as a result of my decision to become a tough guy and put on a tough guy exterior, I became a target for negativity. It wasn't until I was almost sixty years old that this vow/energy changed. I used to almost come to blows with people everywhere I went.

Sometimes I would be at a store and a fistfight would nearly break out. One time in my late thirties, I was coming home from work and decided to go to the store to pick up some items for dinner. I was moving down an aisle when I encountered a man and wife with their two teenage daughters.

The woman was totally blocking the aisle with her and her cart. I asked, "Excuse me. Can you move?" All the people looked at me and they obviously heard and understood me. The lady stared directly at me and didn't move. She continued to talk to her husband. I again politely asked and again, no response. I raised my hands and shoulders in a sort of shrug and asked again.

The daughters spoke up and said, "Mom, this man is trying to get through. Move for him!"

The husband immediately spoke up and said, "She doesn't have to move for anyone! If he wants to make something of it let him try!"

Here I was, trying to be nice and polite, and I was met with total hostility! I immediately had waves of anger come up and was ready to explode into violence. I WOULD NOT LET PEOPLE TREAT ME INHUMANELY ANY MORE!

At once, I imagined my being arrested and news headlines' reading "Prominent businessman arrested in assault of grocery patron." I feared that, if I allowed myself to blow up, I might kill this man. So I bit my tongue and moved backwards down the aisle.

Incidents like this happened often to me. Again, by the grace of God, I never had any serious incidents, although I came VERY close, too many times to count. I now know that I have had a powerful set of guardian angels and/or guides protecting me. Later in this book I will detail one of the many "miracles" I have had as a result of my spiritual quest. This particular miracle relates to how this energetic pattern has changed.

Not all things were negative for me at this time. Although I couldn't hit golf balls, I could putt. This caused a lot of pain, but the doctors told me that it wouldn't damage my arms.

In these years I had such severe pain in my elbows that it was nearly impossible to pick up a gallon of water or brush my teeth.

I used to spend a lot of time at my dad's friend's golf course. It was a neat place. Many touring pros and many aspiring pros practiced there. At least I could get away from school, as I had a car, and I could spend time in the outdoors, which I have always loved.

It was during my second semester, in February, that I met Marla, a girl who worked at this golf course. We started dating. I immediately like her, although I was totally not sure how to act on a date, had almost no self esteem, and was scared stiff.

After a few weeks of dating, she told me that she would be moving to California in April. I was quite distraught at hearing this news.

Any time during my life when I had someone who liked me, they would move. Do you remember that dorky kid I befriended that first day of high school? He was one of the friends I had made who moved soon after we met. The only boy in elementary school that ever truly liked me, and was ridiculed for it, moved to New York after we had been friends only a few months. Again, something in my energy or what I attract made this a common occurrence.

One interesting fact about Marla's imminent departure was that she was moving to Santa Barbara, where I just happened to have many relatives. I had them get her a place. When it came time to move, she had a place already lined up and I had my family to help her out. I also had an excuse to visit her! (We dated for over twelve years, mostly long distance. We have been married for over thirty.)

After my future wife left for California, I was very down. It was at this point in my life that I seriously contemplated suicide. At one point, I had a shotgun out and was thinking that I couldn't go on. *What's the point?* Then I thought of my parents. *What would this do to them?* This is what stopped me. *I couldn't be that selfish!* While thoughts like this continued, from this point on I knew that I wouldn't be able to actually do it.

In what would have been my junior year of college I decided to take the year off of school and work on my golf game. I was now good to go as far as hitting balls, although I still had quite a bit of pain.

My dad's friend, a fairly well-known touring pro, started helping me with my swing. Obviously, after almost five years of not swinging a club I was rusty.

This pro, Dean Refram, knew how well I used to hit the ball. Despite this, he said I needed to revamp my swing, as it wasn't "orthodox." I went along, as I was having difficulty getting my old swing back. After all the time and changes, I had lost my previous intuitive swing.

Golf was why I had a desire to live. It was all based on hate and inferiority. At twenty years of age, I was totally lost. I went back to school my last two years and graduated *Cum*

Laude. The only reason I didn't have a higher grade point average is because of my hatred for certain teachers whom I labeled as bullies. I would not work for someone I judged as a creep. Whenever I had a teacher who was somewhat human, I received an A in his/her class.

I spent the next ten years on a quest for the "perfect swing." I thought my life would be a failure if I couldn't show everyone up. In hindsight, this is not a healthy path to success. During these years, I became even angrier and more hate-filled. I also became very judgmental. One saving grace in all of this was my sense of spirituality, though certain aspects of my spirituality became clouded as I became angry at God for allowing such injustice. I did have an inner knowing however, that somehow was stronger than my hate and uncertainty.

Chapter 3: Beginning My Metaphysical Quest

When I was twelve, my aunt Tina gave me a book titled, How to Relax and Revitalize Yourself, by Murdo MacDonald Bayne. I read this book voraciously. Although it was filled with wisdom, I was attracted to the part where Bayne talks about people who have a magnetism that attracts friends and goodness. This is the exact opposite of what life had given me.

This book became my "personal bible." I would often pick it up and read sections of it. It had a way of soothing me and allowing me to cope with a life I thought of as hell. I used to sit for hours contemplating how Bayne could have come by such wisdom. During the next two decades, I received more books from my aunt and talked with her several times about her own spiritual journey. I came to find out that she was born with extra fingers and was cruelly treated by not only her peers, but her own father.

There were ten children in my father's family. My dad's father was a cruel individual. My grandmother and her children, my aunts and uncles, were impoverished and mistreated by him. My dad often commented that, had it not been for his mother's selfless love, he would have turned out rotten. Instead of his being bitter and showing contempt for the world, he decided to help people and show love. Don't get me wrong; he was tough and sometimes could be cold and heartless. Like me, though, his opinion or judgment of a person would dictate how he would respond to them. Toward his family, my dad (and my mom) were incredibly loving.

The period of my life between the ages of twenty and thirty was a trying time. I was on two simultaneous quests. One was to know God, or as I was now beginning to call it, Universal Consciousness.

I had become jaded with organized religion. *How could religion allow such hypocrisy? What could God be to allow such goings on?* Some of my questions on this front were beginning to be answered by metaphysicians like Bayne.

The other quest was the golf swing. Golf, as I noted earlier, was my way to pay back my abusers. My dad and I used to call it the quest for the Holy Grail.

I really left no stone unturned on either front. I had an incredibly supportive father who was the only person on the planet who had an inkling of what I had gone through. He supported my golf quest without hesitation.

Partly this was because, not only could he could relate to my abuse, he was really the only other person who saw my talent as a golfer. We spent much time together during those years. He was selfless in his devotion to me and my quest. Also, he was a "closet" metaphysician. He was a master at psychology and a consummate optimist.

During this time, I began to become soothed by meditation, introspection, and energetic clearing. Some of my memories were coming back to me, memories which I had forgotten or suppressed because of my childhood experiences.

My future wife came back to Florida after her schooling and we were together for a short time before she got a job in Philadelphia. I was spending the winters in Florida working on my golf. During the summers, I went back to the Chicago area and started working for the family business. Since it was a family business, I had the luxury, and support, to enable me to have a flexible schedule. This schedule allowed a lot of time for golf, and my dad fully supported it.

As noted earlier, I was having a lot of physical discomfort during these years. I embarked on my spruce goose routine of physical readiness. At eighteen, I began running, a fad that caught on tremendously in the 1970s. After a few years, I was running forty miles per week. This lasted until my late thirties, although I have never completely given it up. I have a runner's body and temperament and love the freedom running gives.

In my mid-twenties I also began weight training at a time when this was not done by golfers. The weight training lasted well into my forties. I had to give it up because it really exacerbated the fibromyalgia. (I am the only person I know who had fibromyalgia and trained heavily with weights. I am sure there are other people out there who have done this, but it is usually not considered to be a good idea.)

Throughout my golfing career, my dad and I used to love searching for golf balls. During my years in Florida, especially when I was not able to play due to injury, I would hunt for golf balls. One year when I packed up to go home for summer break I had well over 1000 top brand balls that I had found in a nearby golf course. I had numerous encounters with water moccasins, rattlesnakes, and non-venomous creatures. Once, I had a four-foot alligator take a bite out of my 4 wood!

My dad had been a member of Medinah Country Club since 1958. Medinah is one square mile in size and is a world-renowned golf facility. It has many lakes and creeks running through it, including one that runs for miles in an east-west direction.

The club was built in the late 1920s and was then far "out of town." There was not much development in the area until the early 1970s. Even now there is much forest preserve and undeveloped land nearby.

Dad and I had favorite spots that we would go to, to find lost golf balls. Both he and I harbored an uneasy feeling in two of these spots. It is difficult to explain the feelings, and we never knew of each other's uneasiness until that summer of 1985.

It was not uncommon for us to see large piles of freshwater clam shells along the various waterways. We would comment about this: "It must be raccoons or opossum."

One day that summer, my dad was playing at Medinah with three of his friends. They came up to the then-17th Hole. It was a par three over water with an elevated tee that looked down at the green.

As my dad's foursome walked up to the tee, they noticed a twosome waiting on the tee, as play had backed up. My dad knew the two gentlemen waiting on the tee. All six of these gentlemen were sixty years old or older and were level-headed mature people who, I want to emphasize, had *not* been drinking.

The two men that had been waiting on the tee motioned to my dad and his friends to look at something. As my dad came up to one of these gentlemen, he said, "Al, look down there! We've been watching this thing for the last ten minutes!"

As my dad focused on the area, he could plainly see what looked to be a seven-foot gorilla peering out from one of the trees to the left of the green.

This creature was about 200-300 feet from where my dad and the others were, separated by a creek about fifty feet wide. My dad's location was at an elevation maybe forty feet above the green's level, so they had an excellent view. The creature was about 200 feet to the left of the green as they faced it from the tee.

This area where the creature stood had been thick old growth hardwood forest until that summer.

That year, in order to make the course comply with an upcoming US Open, much of the previous forest had been cleared and a new hole created.

The area to the left of the green had been one of the two areas mentioned previously where my dad and I had those uneasy feelings when we hunted for lost golf balls. Also, this area had never been used before and was a tangled forest of old growth hardwood trees and brush, almost impenetrable, bordered water on one side; it was approximately six acres within the confines of the golf course.

The creek ran under Medinah Road to the west and could have been used as a thoroughfare to a large area of undeveloped land. To the east, the creek ran into Lake Kadijah.

The creature was taking in the construction of the new golf hole. It appeared to be watching a bulldozer leveling land near the present green's location. It was peering out from behind a tree and appeared to be hiding from view. After a while, the twosome who had alerted my dad and his group about the sighting teed off and left. My dad and his group continued to watch the creature for another five or ten minutes.

Suddenly, something startled the creature and it ran off to the left, and with one bound vaulted over a seven to eight-foot fence with barbed wire covering the top foot of the fence. It then bounded over Medinah Road in what my dad described as three big hops, over the two-lane highway, and disappeared into the woods on the other side.

My dad, who never believed in much he couldn't verify scientifically, went on a quest for the next several years to find answers. He even tried to get the other five men who had witnessed the creature to write signed affidavits attesting to what they saw. I believe several of them did; the others refused.

Dad called the police and made inquiries as to whether any animals were lost or had escaped, etc. He canvassed the homes in the area of the sighting, which at that time were few in number. Several people admitted that they often felt uneasy outdoors, which they couldn't explain. They also mentioned a lot of strange noises at night.

He discovered that there was an abandoned quarry in the direction that the creature ran off to and there was also an old abandoned amusement park on the corner of Lake Avenue and Medinah Road, also in that same direction. The park was large, had many abandoned buildings on it, and had been deserted for years. He also queried many of the members of Medinah about possible sightings of an unusual creature.

Not surprisingly, he was met with much ridicule, even from the two men who alerted my dad to the creature's presence and had watched it with him for about ten minutes. My dad was a strong, independent man who never cared what others thought of him, hence the ridicule never dampened his spirits or his zeal to find answers.

Dad told me that this creature was large, and, while it looked like a gorilla, it had no neck and appeared larger that the gorillas he had seen in zoos. He said, "It almost appeared human but was far too large and agile."

He did some research and found out about a creature called a Sasquatch. He made inquiries and eventually contacted a professor at the University of Idaho who was a Sasquatch authority.

This professor found my dad's story to be credible and suggested that he read the book entitled <u>Sasquatch, the Apes Among Us</u>. He told my dad to try and get his account of what happened to the Chicago area newspapers as this would not only make it more known, for possible additional people to come forward, but it may add credibility to his account if it were indeed published.

As a result of my dad's perseverance, *The Chicago Tribune* did publish the story some time later, but the account suggested that my dad and the others were intoxicated, "…as one knows how businessmen on a golf course can be."

In my dad's defense, he took the game very seriously, sometimes winning or losing $1000 or more on a round. Believe me, he never drank while playing, nor would his fellow players risk that kind of money by being intoxicated!

About two years after this occurrence, something even more bizarre happened to solidify the veracity of this story. My dad was having lunch with a friend whom he hadn't talked to in quite a while. This man, Bruce Houdek, was a longtime friend of my dad's and also a childhood friend of the touring pro

Dean Refram, who had revamped my swing during college.

My dad started to tell Bruce of his encounter with the creature. "You'll never believe what I saw out at Medinah!" he exclaimed.

Bruce turned pale and said, "I think I know what you're going to tell me," he said.

"No, you couldn't possibly know!" Dad said, and related the story without interruption from Bruce.

After my dad was done, Bruce rather reluctantly said, "Dean (not me but the touring pro) and I saw the same thing back in 1957."

He told my dad that he had never mentioned this sighting to anyone in the last thirty years.

It seems he and Dean drove out to the fifth hole on the Number 3 course at Medinah. (This was the other location where my dad and I always felt uneasy!) They used Dean's mother's car, a brand-new 1957 Thunderbird, to go out to the fifth hole to try out a new driver Dean had purchased. The hole was a par five, an ideal hole to test out a new driver.

While they were on the tee, they heard a rustling noise and snapping of branches in the nearby woods. They both looked up and saw what appeared to be a gorilla. As they and the creature made eye contact, the creature took off.

Dean yelled, "Let's head it off!" and they got in the car and took off. As Dean was backing out, he still had his driver's door partially open and it struck and hung up on a low concrete culvert wall. Bruce remembered the year of the incident as he remembered how mad Dean's father was at them for damaging the brand-new T-Bird. Bruce related in retrospect how foolish it was for them to go after such a creature -- what would they have done if they ever caught up with it!

I have since done much reading about Sasquatch and have yet to find a more compelling [multiple] eyewitness account of the creature. During some research a couple of years ago, I was able to pull up, on a Sasquatch database (yes, there is such a thing[1]), reference to both my dad's sighting and Bruce's in 1957. I can only assume that my dad must have included Bruce's account with his. I never recall his telling me that, but I think it is the only way that story could have been known.

[1] http://www.communitywalk.com/location/john_green_database__du_page_county_illinois___991012/john_green_database/5152346

Chapter 4: Future Home

Sparing many of the details, I worked on my golf game and spent countless hours practicing, abusing my body in the process. I had been to some of the top golf teachers in the country and studied countless hours of video to improve my technique.

When I was in my early twenties, the pro who had started to revamp my swing realized he had made a terrible mistake. I had lost my "natural" swing and was a shadow of the player I had been in my teens. He felt guilty and didn't know how to help me. If he saw me coming, he would go the other way.

As I searched for my game, I met a young pro from England. His name was Don and he was a godsend. He gave me hope at a time when I needed it. He was/is a great teacher and even though I haven't seen or talked to him in about thirty years, I still think of him as a friend.

He improved my swing and game to the point where he asked me if I would accompany him to Florida and play the mini tour with him. This tour let amateurs play unless there were too many pros in the field for any specific tournament. So we played this tour for a few months and although I didn't play astounding golf, it did give me a boost.

One night, we had returned to our room and Don noticed a book I was reading. It was a copy of <u>The Life and Teachings of the Masters of the Far East</u>. He knew I enjoyed reading, but knew nothing of the subject matter. He asked to read it when I was done, and since I had read it before I immediately gave him the book. I thought *Oh, he'll read a couple of pages and think I'm crazy*. The next morning he told me he had been up most of the night reading it. He was fascinated. He went out and purchased the whole set of four or five books that comprised this series.

Months later, when visiting back home in England, Don's father told him an intriguing story. He, it seems, picked up his son's copy of <u>The Life and Teachings</u> and read it. He had never talked about his war experiences to anyone before. He hadn't even talked about them with his wife.

Don's father opened up about an experience he had during WWII, while stationed in the Syrian Desert. He struck up a friendship with a man he thought was a desert nomad. He would go and have tea with this nomad every Sunday. They talked of many things and the nomad seemed to know much about Don's father; things he couldn't have known.

After several months of these afternoon teas the nomad said that they would never meet again. Don's father quickly explained that he enjoyed the talks and he was not going to be transferred, that they would still be able to meet. The nomad explained that no, this would be their last meeting.

"I want to tell you a few parting words that you must remember," the nomad said. He told Don's father that he would have two children, a boy who would be a world traveler (Don), and a daughter. I don't recall, but he talked about the daughter in specific terms, which years later came true.

He also talked a bit more about Don, things that also came true. The nomad said, "You must remember to not lose hope; remember what I have told you."

A few days later, Don's father's unit was attacked. Many people died and Don's father was critically wounded. They didn't know if he would make it.

Don's father was in terrible pain, so severe that he thought of taking his own life. Over several weeks he made slow progress. He was still despondent and still didn't think he would survive.

He had lost the will to live. One afternoon, a nurse came in and asked if he wanted any tea. Suddenly he remembered what the nomad had told him, that he would go on to have two children and not to lose hope. From this point on Don's father made a quick recovery. He somehow knew the nomad's words were true.

Don also told me that his father had talked about this group of tribesman in the area in Syria where they were stationed. He told of many amazing stories and feats these nomads could perform. One time he witnessed a tank run over one of the tribesman. The tribesman just got up after the incident, totally unscathed. My intuition tells me that these nomads were a group of Sufi masters.

One interesting experience I had right after playing the tour with Don was when I played golf at an exclusive club that bordered Bok Tower, south of Orlando, Florida. I played very well here and felt "seasoned" after playing the tour. When the round was over, I toured the Bok Tower grounds and felt an incredible energy there. There was a sense that I had been there before and I felt a deep reverence in the energy of that place. I only mention this because there have been few places where I have felt this type of sacredness. It is akin to what one feels when in deep meditation.

At the age of thirty, I decided to quit golf. Like so many things in my life, golf had been a bitter disappointment. I felt that it had given me nothing but misery. As with many quests, it was filled with great expectations never fulfilled.

And there was Marla to consider. We had dated for almost thirteen years. She never complained, although I am sure she must have thought I was crazy. We married when I was thirty years old. I decided at that point that I would totally give golf up. I wasn't interested even in continuing to play for fun. I started to work full-time for the family business and focus on a home and family.

My wife and I had a dream to have some land where we could have horses, a big garden, and solitude. Since an early age I held an incredible love of horses. Our family traveled to Colorado in 1964 and 1966. We stayed at a "dude ranch" where I fell in love with horses, pine forests, and mountains. One of my first horses there was an incredible Appaloosa gelding named Rooster. He was blind in one eye and given to the more seasoned riders. Although I was very young I was able to handle him.

I never knew such beauty existed in the world. It brought back faint memories of some forgotten dream. Since my first visit to Colorado in 1964 I have always wanted to live in the mountains. Marla had spent a lot of her youth on her grandfather's farm and had horses where she grew up in Florida. She loved the same things as I.

We had begun looking for property before we got married. We would drive north of Chicago trying to find something that fit our needs. At this time I started working energetically on my vision of our future property. I had even started formulating my dream home/farm in my mind. Using some metaphysical techniques I had learned, and also specifically visualizing what I wanted, I had a precisely detailed picture of what I wanted.

We had started to look in the northern Chicago suburbs and gradually kept moving north until we were looking in Wisconsin. This was largely due to the price of farmland.

In October of 1987 a friend of my dad's came into the office. He told me about a farm he had seen that bordered, of all things, a golf course. He drove to the property and was captured by something intangible. Marla and I drove up that next weekend and found that it was farther west than we had ever looked before. We had put limits on how far out we would buy, as I needed to commute to work.

One perceived negative about the farm was the distance to work. The other negative was that it covered 145 acres. We had been looking at a maximum of fifty. This was almost three times that size!

We clocked the drive time to work and found we could make the commute (with no traffic) in thirty-five minutes. The price was attractive -- comparable to fifty acres in Illinois. We made an appointment with a realtor and looked at the property. There was a special energy about it.

After touring the property the big negative now was not the price, the location, or the size. The negative was that it was a junkyard of old equipment, rundown buildings, and overgrown pastures. Not only was all this junk unusable, it would cost a lot of money to clear it. Plus, we would have to build our own home, as the one on the property was not fit to live in.

My parents, who were to help us buy a property, had been out of town for two weeks. When they returned home, my dad seemed negative about it, but he did agree to look at it. He and my mom went up a few days later.

My dad was a savvy businessman and I knew he knew a lot more about property than I. Due to his initial reaction and knowing how picky he could be, I was sure he wouldn't like it, but when he came back from looking at it, he was glowing. He said, "You've *got* to buy this!"

So we started negotiating on price and found out the property had been for sale for several years, mainly due to the fact that it contained so much junk. After much negotiating we wound up buying the property at what turned out to be the lowest price point for farmland of this type, near this location, in the last forty years.

I told my wife before we bought it that it would take us ten years to get it in the shape we wanted it. It turned out to be almost exactly ten years to revitalize it, but we managed it. I could see in this property everything that I had ever wanted in a place to live, other than that it wasn't near the Rockies.

I could also envision what I would turn it into. I saw it as a blank canvas, one that I would paint my masterpiece on. Another interesting fact about the property was that the farm had been in the owner's family for about a hundred years. It turns out that he had his main home a couple of blocks from where my childhood home was. I used to jog by his house every day for years!

We bought the property in April, 1988 and broke ground for our new home in July, 1989. Those days, I went up to the land every free moment and began the long process of clearing fence lines, removing large boulders and cleaning up literally tons of junk. Marla was still working full time, yet she found time to come up and do many of the chores that needed to be done.

We sold our condominium in the Chicago suburbs and moved in with my parents in order to have money to start many of the costly projects that needed to be done before we could build. I would go up almost every night after work and work until it was dark. Marla and I became proficient at running heavy machinery and also doing much of the maintenance such machines require.

We gradually cleared the land and picked a new home site. At this time I began to do a lot of energy work clearing the land, and specifically on our new home site which was on a hill overlooking a six-acre pond. The first few brush strokes were complete on my canvas, but it was still far from the masterpiece I had envisioned.

Chapter 5: Psychic Unfolding

About this time, I began to feel a lot of energy about the land. I also started to have a knowing that this land was blessed and sacred, that it was on some sort of special energetic ley lines. I didn't know much about such things, but my years of studying metaphysics taught me that such things existed, and I had learned to trust my intuition on this. There were so many ideas floating around in my mind as to how I would turn this land into my dream!

I have been told by several intuitives/psychics that there is a Native American spirit living on the land, the spirit of a shaman or medicine man. One that blesses the area, helps provide abundance, and is pleased at how we've treated the land. I have "connected" with this spirit many times and have asked for help with various projects.

In fact, Thomas Pecora, whom I mentioned earlier, told me that this land had been a native American burial site, going far back in time.

Thomas is very attuned to Native American energy as he was mentored by Wallace Black Elk. You can read his fascinating story[2] on line.

As I worked with Bayne's books, my inner knowing and early childhood experiences began to crystallize. I studied many books by Bayne, Joel Goldsmith, Ruby Nelson, and Eastern works like The Bhagavad Gita and works by Yogananda. I have also been fascinated by The Urantia Book, and I am particularlydrawn to Jean Klein's concept of "There is no object." I have also extensively studied Hermetics, Kabalah, Sufism, and Christian Mysicism.

In the early 1980s I found a program by Jonathan Parker, *Pathways to Mastership*. I believe I saw an ad in a yoga magazine with a course description that captivated me. This, I thought, was exactly what I needed.

Over the next decade, I purchased much of what Parker had for sale. He was a prolific purveyor of courses on cassette tape (and now as MP3 files). I leaned many things from his courses that I hadn't seen anywhere else.

The best way I could describe his work was that he seemed to distill the best of many teachers and teachings into a concise formula that, for me, produced results. As far as I remember, his work was the only metaphysical material produced on cassette tape at that time. The tape medium was innovative to me and Parker's voice had an almost meditative effect on me. In addition, he featured the most beautiful music I had ever heard up to that point in my life. It had an other-worldly quality that put me in an altered state.

When I was a child, I had an unusual taste in music. I was never into popular music as most of my peers were. It wasn't until I was in college that I really listened to pop. The reason for this was that I spent a lot of time driving and it was one of the few choices available. I wasn't necessarily drawn to classical music, but I did have an early fascination for harp music.

I remember wanting to meet Jonathan and pick his brain for information that would help me on my spiritual quest. He seemed to have what I was wanting. When I called his office, someone told me that he didn't do consultations or personal sessions at that time. So, I felt I had to be content with his tapes. In the meantime, I began meditating more, finding what I would describe as ethereal music, and studying whatever I could get my hands on regarding metaphysics.

Years later, in my own workshops people would comment on the music I would play. They wanted to purchase it and learn where I found music like this.

Throughout the late '80s and '90s I began listening to "New Age" music. I even helped personally sponsor a radio show in Milwaukee which played this type of world new age music. I now have an extensive collection of this type of music dating from the late '80s through the present.

During these days I longed for freedom -- freedom from the body, which was constantly giving me physical pain, freedom of my monkey mind, freedom from my anger and negative emotions, freedom from my dreams of revenge, and freedom of the ego.

From an early age I had feelings of not wanting to die in the conventional sense. I believed, from early childhood memories, that I could ascend similarly to what Jesus did. Even with my upbringing as Catholic, I knew this was possible.

In 1992, the year that we had our second child and had been living in our new house for two years (and more than ten years after I had my first encounter with the work of Parker), I was astounded to hear that he was going to give a workshop. My brother, to whom years earlier I had given *Pathways to Mastership,* wanted to go with me. It was to happen in, of all places, Santa Barbara. (Over the years, I have purchased countless *Pathways* sets and given them away, sometimes to total strangers.)

The workshop was amazing. It marked a turning point in my metaphysical life. I went to all, or almost all, of the workshops Parker did for the next seven years. During this time he introduced me to energy healing. I found that I had a real talent for this type work. To date I have performed many healings and readings, by my best guess, well in to the 3000s. I also, have never charged for my work. My payment is my service to help alleviate people's suffering of which I am so well aware.

Throughout much of the nineties there was a core group of Parker followers. Parker mentioned that this group was part of a soul group that had known each other before this present incarnation and agreed to meet up and be "taught" by Parker. I definitely felt this to be true. There were many neat people in this group, from all over the world.

As I continued to follow the works and teachings of Parker I continued delving into the works of others. I did the home study course from Self Realization Fellowship (Kryia Yoga), which took several years to complete, and got much more involved in meditation, experiencing traveling in meditation; I reached points where I could hear things and feel the Profound Oneness that is often talked about by meditators. Despite my otherworldly experiences, I still thought of myself as not intuitive at all. While at many of Parker's early workshops I didn't seem to connect as others seemed to.

At one of these early workshops, I met a young lady, Lorraine, and we started talking about our spiritual experiences. As I explained my perceived lack of intuition, she mentioned that a young man she worked with would be a perfect fit for me and my quest. She assured me that he would be able to unlock my abilities. Lorraine mentioned that her mentor, Larry, didn't work with other people as he was consumed with his own metaphysical work and as a film director in Hollywood. Nevertheless, she felt certain that he would make an exception for me. She agreed to pass my name along to Larry, and if he were interested, I could expect to hear from him.

As usual, that workshop where I met Lorraine was great. I returned home to my family, farm, business, and my meditations. Several months went by, and I had pretty much forgotten about Larry, Lorraine's mentor. One morning at work I received a phone call. (I make it a rule for my secretary not to screen my calls, except for rare occasions. I feel it is rude to not at least let people introduce themselves to me. I always maintained an open door/phone policy throughout my business career even though many people thought I was nuts to do this.)

I took the call and the person on the other end said, "Do you work at a Buick Dealership?" I was a little perplexed. *Yes I do, and why would someone call and ask for me specifically where I work if he doesn't know that? Very strange.*

I replied, "Yes I do. Why do you want to know?" He told me that his name was Larry, and Lorraine had asked him to call me. In addition, he said, "My father works at another Buick dealership in Chicago."

It turns out that our fathers had known each other for something like twenty years! He continued to tell me that although he didn't take on new clients, he would make an exception for me. We wound up working together for about the next seven years, though it took about three years before we ever met in person, as he lived in California.

During the years when I worked with Larry, I still attended almost all of the workshops Parker put on. I had some transformative experiences in those workshops. These, plus working with Larry built my confidence in my own metaphysical abilities, along with being a lot of fun.

There were many interesting people in those seminars, all seemingly hungering for answers that mainstream society could not answer. One standout I remember was a girl who was still in high school and probably about sixteen years old. She came to that particular workshop because she had heard about Parker's teachings. Since her earliest memories, she had seen auras around everyone, including many inanimate objects. I recall her mentioning that she had to sit in the front row of her classrooms as if she didn't, people's auras would interfere with her ability see to the board. She found many answers in that workshop and was greatly relieved by Parker's explanations and teachings. She also gave readings of everyone's auras!

Another instance that I found incredible at the time had to do with another "student" of Jonathan's. This lady was a professional psychic.

Her name was Pat. I had up to that point never encountered a professional psychic. Several years after this encounter, I regularly began to see psychics, mediums, and healers to further my esoteric quest.

Pat and I were having lunch and she mentioned to me that there were two people standing behind me and that they were my spirit guides. She perfectly described my grandparents on my mother's side, both deceased. She then told me that I was thinking of selling my family business and gave me a dollar amount that I expected to receive from the sale. Now, this lady had no knowledge of me and I had never discussed this possible sale with anyone other than close confidents. The amount was exact.

A few days later, Jonathan was leading a guided meditation. In all my years of going to workshops or participating in guided meditations, Jonathan Parker was the best at leading them. During this meditation I clearly saw, in my mind's eye, an angel. He was a huge golden colored angel around eight feet tall standing directly behind me. He stood behind me, like a guard, for the entire meditation.

I believe this was the earliest "vision" I had as an adult, and it was certainly one of the most vivid. After the meditation, wanting some sort of validation, I asked Parker if he had seen anything during the meditation. (Parker often would move energy around during these events and was acutely aware of the subtle energies happening during these sessions.) He told me that there were many spirits and angels around. I asked specifically if he had seen any near me and he told me he didn't remember anything specific, but he suggested I talk to Pat who was at the opposite end of the large room. Parker had noticed that she was "very aware of the goings on in this meditation."

I then asked Pat if she noticed anything in particular around me during the meditation. She said rather matter-of-factly, "The only thing I remember around you was an eight foot tall golden angel standing behind you." There were many other memorable events at those years I spent with Parker. He put me on a stable foundation for my later work.

Larry worked with me over the phone. I didn't know what to expect from him. A week or two went by after our initial call. Then he called me at home, and the first thing he told me was to relax and he would "go into my energy."

Now this night was unusual in that I had an upset stomach. I almost never experienced an upset stomach. I didn't mention anything about myself at all, and Larry didn't ask me any questions, either.

The first comment Larry said after he "moved in to my energy" was, "Oh, you have an upset stomach."

I was shocked. *How could he know? He was over 2000 miles away, couldn't see me and had no knowledge of me other than what Lorraine had told him.* Since it was rare for me to have an upset stomach, it wasn't something that someone could have guessed from my history. When I questioned Larry about his knowing he simply said that this was part of what he intended to teach me.

Up to this point in my life, I had never had any personal "sessions" with anyone regarding the esoteric. I had mostly kept my spiritual search to myself, being embarrassed and not wanting to be open to ridicule. Going to Parker's seminars was the first time I had ever let others (other than immediate family and my friend Don) know that I was interested in this sort of thing. I had never gone to a psychic, intuitive, medium, etc.

As I worked with Larry over the next several years, things started to really open up for me. He held a space for me that enabled me to more easily travel and "channel" my higher self. I had tremendous healings during this period of time. I gained more confidence and started to have a knowing of what other metaphysicians had talked about for hundreds or even thousands of years. I also experienced many healings revolving around what could best be termed "attachment or entity releasing."

I questioned Larry about how he became interested in this sort of work. To the best of my recollection, he explained to me that as a child of around ten, his mother took him to Egypt. While walking in the marketplace he had a powerful vision. He knew without a doubt that he had lived there before. I believe he told me that his second sight began to open up as a result. Upon returning home he read the works of Carlos Castaneda. He got into intuitive work with a teacher in New York and started to develop his skill by applying metaphysics to the work of psychologist Eugene Gendlin.

After several years I became convinced that Larry's work would be a boon to mankind. In retrospect the work he and Parker were doing was at least a decade or two ahead of its time. I had experienced such tremendous growth over what I considered to be a relatively short time.

I asked Larry to teach me what he knew. He hemmed and hawed and eventually said yes. He would take me on as his "apprentice," his first ever. He cautioned me regarding many things, trying to dissuade me. I still wanted to move ahead. For the next several years our friendship grew, as did my abilities. When we started, he would be the reader and he would have me tag along for the ride, so to speak. Eventually we started swapping sessions with each other. There were many what I consider to be amazing healings and knowledge gained during this time.

One instance of this was where Larry was in my energy. He lit up a particular aspect of my being. He told me he saw an attachment, or entity, in my field. This entity was somewhat difficult to track down as it kept hiding. I, also, had learned how to spot these and track them from Larry's teachings. This time he was the tracker. I had learned how to see most of what he was seeing in my field.

Occasionally we would have different "takes" on things. I learned that people each have their own set of filters which color what they see or how they would interpret certain things. Once Larry tracked it and "isolated" the attachment, I was easily able to move into the energy of it. This was a highly developed energy. There are many degrees of sophistication with the aberrations that may exist in one's energy bodies. They can range from thought forms or beliefs, which to me usually appear as clouds, colors or even feelings, to highly crystallized structures having much complexity.

This one began to speak. It said that it had served me (the personality) for over 58,000 years. Larry started to ask it many different questions. It started talking (through me) about quantum physics and how it related to our spiritual searching, and many other things that I had no knowledge of. I experienced, at that moment, a complete understanding of what it was saying. On one level I could hear Larry and understand how he was working. On another level I could understand concepts like quantum physics that were totally foreign to me.

On yet another level, although I was in a deeply altered state, I could write notes on what was being said. This was a skill that I learned from working with Larry. He was famous for saying to "take copious notes," although usually this would occur after one was done with a session and more grounded. I now believe that what it was talking about is similar to what physicists are now calling The Emergence Theory. (Check out this video[3])

Larry had different techniques of releasing entities or whatever energy was hindering one's growth. The entity talked of these advanced concepts, along with other things through me for a couple of hours, as Larry was fascinated with what it was saying. This time this entity was "convinced" to move into the light. I had a strong emotion of sadness as it left. I later realized that since it had been with me through many incarnations, it was in some sense, a friend that was leaving. As it left I had a sensation of hundreds of angels working with us and also of a heavy blanket being lifted off of me. It was a palpable feeling.

I had many releases like this during the years I worked with Larry. One other interesting past life clearing had to do with a lifetime in which

I was a king in a northern country. I was banished to a cold wasteland as I had been usurped. I recalled dying of exposure. As Larry was working with me, I felt the numbing cold in my present body. After the session ended, I needed to take a hot shower to warm up!

All of the thought forms, entities and attachments that were released enabled me to become much clearer and really developed my sense of intuition. I realized that I had always been highly intuitive. Being intuitive was so natural to me that it was like not seeing the forest for the trees. I found that I didn't need to do any processes; just let the information flow.

I also realized that I seem to channel my "higher self" rather than guides. More often than not, I believe, this is just a matter of interpretation by the channel, although the clearer I became I could tell the difference. I found out that I had the ability to fairly easily trace past life threads back to root causes. This ability would often manifest while I was doing my work. I had too many experiences with Larry to recount here, but I must share one that still blows my mind.

We were in Sedona during a Parker seminar. Larry wanted to eat at his favorite place, a Japanese restaurant. While we were waiting for our food to be delivered Larry instructed me to hold my cup of tea. He told me to move in to the energy of the tea.

As I had learned earlier from him, everything is energy. If there is nothing but God, then everything is God, even a stone. In fact, my first assignment when I started to work with Larry was to move in to the energy of plants.

These exercises took over a year before Larry was confident in my abilities. In other words, all I did in my first year with Larry was to read the energy of plants. He would not let me move on until I was extremely proficient at this. So, at Larry's instruction, I moved in to the energy of the tea. I had done similar things before, but this time was different. I found myself becoming the tea. Years later I was writing channeled poetry and this came to me totally out of the blue. I feel it captures the essence of that experience.

Turn the page...

Sweet Tea

He told me to drink from the cup.
Trusting him, I did, and I knew…
I knew from whence the plant grew.
I knew how it became sweet.
I truly knew how to savor.
I was the rocky soil that had nurtured
 it
And even the cup that held its flavor.
I felt the warm winds caressing my
 leaves.
I was the plant itself.
That I could know these things is
 a testament
To the One Energy.
I will never forget that lesson.
It was a mile marker on the way home.
The memory has helped me many times,
 especially when I feel all alone.
We are but leaves of the One Great
 Plant,
One great blissful energy.
Harness this gift of feeling
And you too will experience
The Oneness of all creation.

Upon contemplating this experience for years, it occurred to me how few people experience their own selves in such a way, let alone experience total Oneness with something seemingly outside one's self. This experience opened a door for me that in later years allowed me to go beyond Lester Levenson's I AM *you* to I AM *that*. I will talk about this more later.

During the 1990s, I sort of came out of the closet regarding my passion for spirituality. I began to go to different seminars by various teachers and to read more books.

In the late 1990s, I graduated from my apprenticeship with Larry. About this time he was involved in a movie production. He was going to put together a movie deal in which he needed investors. Larry and I had a vision whereby we would build upon the success of this movie and gradually start producing movies of a highly spiritual nature. Much of our work together was directed at improving not only ourselves but the world. Since we were both involved in metaphysics this would be our focus. About this time, the movie, WHAT DREAMS MAY COME came out. Although this movie didn't fit totally into what we had envisioned, it did represent a paradigm shift that we thought was positive.

Larry and I put a tremendous amount of energy and time visualizing what we wanted for this current movie (ours) to do and be. We felt we had all our bases covered and I put my faith totally with Larry.

I managed to get a lot of the financing through family and friends. I had put my trust into Larry, and my friends had put their faith in me. It turned out the movie was a disaster on many fronts, but it was a great learning lesson for me. I realized that a successful outcome wasn't exactly what I thought it should be.

Also at this time I embarked to "change the world" on another front. I decided, with Larry's blessing, to start training people to do what Larry had trained me to do. Through various means and contacts I found a handful of people living across the United States that jumped at the chance to be "trained." These were people I had worked with over the previous few years. As part of my apprenticeship with Larry, he wanted me to facilitate sessions with others, as he had done with me. I wanted to start with this core group and refine my teaching abilities, then take on new apprentices; certain ones of these would be given my blessing to, in turn, train their own.

I envisioned a worldwide network of healers helping humanity!

Over the course of the next several years I would come home from work, eat dinner, spend a few minutes with family, and then usually by 7 p.m. I would be on the phone with my trainees, four or five days per week. These training sessions would commonly run well past midnight. I wanted to train a network of healers, who would, one person at a time, transform the world.

Again, my vision of creating a better world fell flat. I decided not to charge for these sessions, which in hindsight was a mistake. Generally speaking, people value what they pay for and I feel most of the people I tried to train took advantage of me. After a couple of years, I decided to quit this goal. The people I picked just weren't as dedicated as I was. Also, I was really burned out by not getting enough sleep during those years.

In 1999 I started to do work with something called Radiant Heart Work. I resonated with Sharon Wendt, who started this work and wrote a book about it. She worked in what I considered to be a similar way to Larry's. It was at one of her weekend retreats that two things really made an impression on me. The first *ahha!* I had was that I finally realized just how good my intuitive abilities were. As a result of my childhood I needed a lot of validation!

One day, Sharon broke our workshop into one-on-one groups. We were to "read" each other and then debrief on what had transpired. I quickly went into my partner's energy. I felt a blockage or "thought form" in her field. As Larry had trained me to do, I traced it back to its origins. I had developed a real talent for tracing cords of things back in to past lives.

In this instance, I told the woman a story of why she was frustrated and sad in this life. It had to do with the fact that she lived in the American South during the days at the time of, or a little before the Civil War.

Her father in that lifetime was extremely overbearing and possessive. He used to lock his daughter in her room almost constantly. She was not permitted to go outside or fraternize with anyone. I went into more details which I will spare here. During the debriefing, I asked my partner what she thought about what I had told her. Her face turned white and she said that about a year earlier she had been to an internationally known psychic whose name I don't remember. She related that this psychic had related the same story to her, almost verbatim. I thus had a confirmation about my abilities that one doing this type of work seldom gets. I was finally starting to move out of my feelings of ineptitude and worthlessness regarding my psychic abilities.

I gave another interesting reading at that workshop to a different woman. I don't remember all of the details except for one key thing: I told her that I saw a white star in her third eye. It was vivid and contained a lot of energy. After the session, we debriefed and she told me that a few years earlier she had a dream whereby a man in white robes came to her. She didn't remember many of the details; however he placed something on her forehead. She said, "Maybe what you saw was that?"

Recently she was paging through a magazine and saw a picture of that same man. He was "some famous yogi." Immediately I knew it was Yogananda. Even though I had studied Yogananda's Kriya Yoga extensively, I had never heard of anything like the white star that I saw. Months later I was reading something from Self Realization Fellowship (Yogananda's school) and it mentioned that in deep meditation, Kriya Yoga disciples sometimes see a white star in their foreheads!

During that same weekend I had another interesting encounter. There were about fifteen people at the workshop. Seven of the group knew each other and all were Reiki masters. They had encountered another woman from the seminar who was in great distress. They asked if I would like to see them work. I said yes.

They stretched the patient out on a table. To me they seemed unfocused and unable to come to a consensus as to how to proceed. At this point the patient became very upset. She was in a lot of pain and was panicking. The "masters" didn't know what to do. The energy just won't flow, they exclaimed.

I asked if I could intervene, as I felt I could help. The masters didn't have much choice as the client said yes. They reluctantly moved and let me have access to their patient. I quickly did my "thing," so to speak. I felt an energy blockage running down her right side. I intuited that it had to do with a childhood trauma she suffered at the hand of her father. I asked her about this incident and she confirmed that this was true and gave a few more details.

Then I ran energy down her right side and cleared the blockage. By acknowledging the abuse by her father, the crystallized energy was allowed to break up. The Rieki masters were amazed. They asked what modality I used in this healing. I replied it was a combination of many things that I had learned, and it was what I thought was needed at that time. They walked away in a huff without asking any further questions.

I could not understand how someone could witness such a profound healing and not want to learn all the information they could about the modality. Instead, they were jealous! This was the second thing that was reinforced at that seminar; that I possessed an extraordinary healing ability.

As a side note, this encounter really crystallized something for me. I have found that many people I encounter in life have what I would call an unwillingness to see many of the things that would help them most. This unwillingness is more not wanting help than anything else. They have a sort of spiritual superiority whereby they will not ask for help, and feel that they know better than the "other guy." In most cases the ego won't allow another to be more experienced or adept than itself in certain areas. Then they often wonder why they are stuck!

For me, I have found this to be a danger, and will regularly call up metaphysicians, even people I have never heard of, and book a paying session with them. I usually pick these from many lists found in many places and pick one that feels right to me. I can usually see a light around their name(s). I will usually book three or four sessions yearly this way, even though I have many friends who would work with me with a simple phone call.

Often in my experience, a session like this will put me into a new paradigm. Not only have I experienced this in metaphysics, but in many aspects life as well. I am a perfectionist by nature and often feel that I can do anything better than anyone else. Over the years, I have learned to ask for help or an opinion on how I may accomplish my task differently than I might do it. With my years of automobile experience, there were dozens of instances of people I knew and interacted with that would buy a car, have repairs done etc. and never ask for my opinion. I have had many instances of people buying cars that I carried and never mentioned it to me and bought or serviced it elsewhere. I never really cared, but it surprised and sometimes annoyed me that they wouldn't at least ask for advice on these matters. This sometimes led to some terrible mistakes!

I have learned to welcome and solicit advice from whoever I think might know something I may be missing (which is usually everybody lol). Then it's up to me to weigh the facts and make the decision. I would much rather have more facts than fewer, more knowledge rather than less. I don't want to miss the trees for the forest. Yes, I stated that oppositely but correctly.

One area during the '80s through the '90s that I was interested in was astral projection. I read the works of Robert Monroe and practiced various techniques for quite a while. While I was never generally interested in "phenomena," I was interested in this aspect of metaphysics. I think because I knew that I traveled during the night and Monroe's descriptions of many things he saw in the astral fit my own idea of such things.

I practiced with little result, but not zero results. One night around Christmas in the late '90s I was sick in bed with the flu. My family and I were scheduled to visit my family about half an hour away. I had a fever of 103 and obviously couldn't go, but I knew the kids really wanted to exchange gifts and see their extended family.

With much reluctance but at my insistence, my wife left me home alone in bed with plenty of water etc. at my bedside. I also had the TV on although I couldn't concentrate at all since I was feverish and felt literally like I was going to die.

At one point I found myself in a realm with spectacular vividness. I felt great and extremely light. The atmosphere would be comparable to viewing an old movie on a bad print (everyday reality) to a 4k enhanced color movie (astral). I knew I was conscious, and I also knew I was not on the earth plane anymore. Always having had an interest in the astral and projecting thought forms there, I often felt I sort of knew the lay of the land. I made the conscious decision to explore this realm while retaining my "waking" consciousness. I really wanted to take advantage of this opportunity!

The land was exquisite. It was extremely lush and colorful. I saw snow-covered mountains in the distance and yet there were palm trees, green grass, flowers and Spanish moss on some of the trees. It had a Northern feel and look to the land yet it had many features only found in the South in our 3-D reality. I saw a beautiful tree in the distance and thought to myself that I would like to examine this tree close up. Immediately I was at the trunk of the tree, as thought seemed to transport me there. After a while of investigation I thought myself to the foot of the mountains. I then seemed to float on a path and saw spectacular homes. I seemed to know that some of these residences belonged to friends and relatives that had passed.

One home in particular lay up in the foothills and it fascinated me. I immediately knew it was the home of my golf pro friend Dean Refram, who had passed a few years prior. I continued to explore and all of a sudden I woke with a start and felt terrible, back in bed with a high fever and headache.

I knew what had just happened was not a dream, but real. Interestingly, I had really noticed and explored some of the trees in that astral realm. As I will note below, I have planted hundreds of trees and seemed to know instinctively which species would do well in specific areas of my property. I have always loved trees!

As I was lying in bed recounting my incredible experience, a TV show came on. It was an animated version of "The Man Who Planted Trees." I had never seen or read anything about this man before. This story has since become one of my favorites and I have recommended it to many over the intervening years. Another strange coincidence! It is difficult to convey but I know that this experience was not a dream. It has to date been the only time that I can honestly say I experienced astral projection while retaining total awake consciousness.

Related to my interest in astral projection is the following story. In the late 1980s, as part of my quest to be physically fit, I hired a personal trainer named Ed. For years we worked out and became friends. During the 1990s as I gradually became more open in my metaphysical quest, Ed started to ask me questions about meditation and other metaphysical topics.

One day he pulled me aside, speaking seriously. "Dean, I have something very troubling to talk to you about." He described to me that almost every night he had trouble falling asleep. He said it was because he was deathly afraid of dying. Every night while in bed he would experience himself "leaving his body." He could pass through solid objects and float like an untethered helium balloon.

He told me that as he would approach the ceiling of his room he would struggle. He felt that if he would pass through the ceiling he would be lost, never again being able to get back to his body.

As he described the experience to me, which had been going on for many years, he was truly terrified. He asked if I could shed any light on this phenomenon, as he had never heard of such goings-on. I told him that I was indeed familiar with this, as it had been described by Monroe and many others. Ed couldn't believe his ears. He never thought anyone had ever experienced something like this. As I described what was happening to him, he became greatly relieved. I also gave him some resources that he could look into as well as some techniques to enable him to more easily control this phenomenon. I also told him of ways to "trace his cord" back to his body if he ever felt fear in becoming lost.

Late in 1999 I decided to quit Parker. I felt that he had taught me all he could. Also, about the same time, I lost touch with Larry. The movie deal along with my completing my training pretty much ended our session work and personal relationship. Again, I felt he taught me all he could. In both cases it was time to move on.

By the year 2000, I received tremendous validation of my abilities. I realized that while I would tell people many things they had heard before, I also would come up with many things that others would not have gotten for them. I believe all intuitives have filters which color their perceptions. My filters seem to be unique indeed. I realized that I had a different take on things specifically suited to an individual's healing on many levels. I have been told by many intuitives that I carry a formula which is outside the normal paradigm but works extremely well, and I have used this ability in my own world to accomplish many things that others attribute to pure luck. If people are willing to be open to new ways of doing things, they can truly live up to their potential. We all have this uniqueness, though most of us won't take the chance.

Looking back as I write this book it beomes evident to me that the 1990s were a blessed time for me. At age forty I decided to do two things that I had wanted to do since childhood. One was to get a really nice telescope and the other was to play the harp.

I knew nothing about either, but I had always loved the sky and stars and, curiously, harp music. I started taking harp lessons with a talented teacher named Anne, and then bought my first telescope. I took lessons from Anne for fifteen years and took my passion for the stars into the hobby of astrophotography. I have become so interested in astrophotography that I constructed an observatory on my farm.

Marla and I built our dream home. We turned the land into what people in our area refer to as one of the most beautiful properties around. We put in miles of fence, grew large gardens every year, put in an orchard, and got our horses. I also planted hundreds of beautiful trees; over thirty different varieties.

I began doing chainsaw art in the late '90s as I became proficient at using chainsaws from clearing acres of brush from our farm. Also, we had our children, Sarah and Andy, and raised them in their formative years in a rarefied atmosphere of love and nature.

The year 2000 approached and I was still hungry to know God, myself, and find more answers. At this point in my life I had established my sanctuary at the farm. The work of art was now complete, although still expanding in beauty!

[2] www.thomaspecora.com/family.html
[3] www.quantumgravityresearch.org/portfolio/what-is-reality-movie

Chapter 6: Past Lives

During the '90s several profound things happened to me along with all of the previously mentioned life events. As I gradually honed my esoteric skills I found myself able to do "automatic writing."

While in an altered state I would write some prose and a lot of poetry. Also, as I "traveled" during my meditations I had what I consider to be an amazing experience and life lesson.

I had quit golf in the mid-1980s, never wanting to resume. In the mid-'90s, during a meditation, I received a download about the golf swing. I now knew exactly what I needed to do to have the perfect swing. I was "instructed" as to what was the secret to distance, accuracy, and repeatability.

In retrospect, I had so completely let go of the need to be a great golfer that the Universe now decided to let me know the secret. It all had to do with releasing my attachments. I told my dad about this as he was the only one who knew how much I had gone through to be a great golfer, and also appreciated my spiritual quest.

He asked me what I would do with this knowledge. I replied that I have to prove what I received would work. *Why would the universe give me such information?* Over the next several months I started to hit balls again. I pulled my clubs out of mothballs and found that after a short time I had my old ability back, along with my putting stroke which I had long since lost.

My dad invited me out to test it on a course. He knew many of the pros in the Chicagoland area and could play at many an area course with just a phone call. We went out and I birdied the first two holes after not having played for about eight years. Over the course of that year we played about fifteen times. I was hitting the ball consistently 300+ yards straight down the middle. My irons were phenomenal, although I found that I was usually only hitting short irons into most greens. I also was putting as well as ever.

Once I had proven my knowledge I lost my ability to want to continue. I did have a notion that maybe I was meant to teach someone this knowledge. Interestingly enough, my dad informed a tour player he knew (not the same one from Florida previously mentioned) about my incredible knowledge of the swing. He even took several lessons from me. I thought this might be the opening the Universe wanted me to follow. It turned out not to be the case.

Another extraordinary thing that happened was regarding a childhood fascination I had. Around the age of ten I heard about the famous aviatrix Amelia Earhart. Many people upon learning about her life and disappearance find it a fascinating story. With me, it was more than that. There was something there that I couldn't explain.

It wasn't until the mid-'90s that I had ever thought about having a reading by a psychic or medium. I thought why I would do such a thing when I had people in my life like Larry and Jonathan Parker. I had never thought about past lives in terms of it being interesting or fascinating, other than how one could heal from it.

Around 1995, my office manager came up to me and made a suggestion for our annual Christmas party. Every year my brothers and I would host what I would describe as a lavish party for a small company such as ours. Some years we had people who had appeared on *The Tonight Show* as entertainment. This year her suggestion was to hire a psychic as entertainment. She had no idea of my metaphysical interests so this was totally her idea. I replied that I didn't have a clue as to who might be good, etc. She said she would do all the legwork and find the right person.

Several weeks went by and she was convinced she found a good one. The psychic agreed to have me and my dad interview her. We went over and we were both amazed at what she came up with. We told her about our party and she suggested we hire a total of three psychics to entertain at our party.

We managed to find two others and the party eventually took place. One of the psychics told me about a past life of mine and that it had a big influence on this life. I had traced many threads of my own past lives before but I was intrigued on this one. Usually when I traced back energies into past lives I would not get specifics about who I was. I had the goal of releasing energy, not exploring specifics. These psychics had a different modality than I was used to. After the party was over, I asked the first psychic we had hired who she thought was really good in terms of the psychic population in general and she told me about Esther Hicks.

Esther Hicks and her channeled being, Abraham, were still relatively new. She still did individual phone readings. I booked a session with her, where I asked about several things including if I had had a previous lifetime in America in the Twentieth Century.

Since early childhood I have had fleeting images of a lifetime during that period. I had also had a knowing that I came back rather soon. I really wasn't sure what this meant, however it would explain some of my early childhood feelings of being very tired and not wanting to be on this plane. Other "memories" I had were images of driving a 1930s era auto and a knowing that I was in the Pacific theater during World War II.

Abraham told me that I did indeed have a lifetime in the first half of the Twentieth Century. He said that I was a writer "of some specific note." When pressed for a name he couldn't come up with one. This was interesting.

I had long recognized my own talent for *writing, and enjoyed it. Could this be some sort of carryover?* He also told me of another notable lifetime in America, one around the Revolutionary War period. Again, there was a lifetime of note.

This piqued my curiosity immensely. I had to wait months for another reading with Esther as she was becoming more popular by the day. I did have another reading with her and she wasn't able to shed any more light on the lifetimes in question.

One last question I asked at this session had fascinated me since childhood. "Whatever happened to Amelia Earhart?"

Abraham answered with a question. "Why do you want to know?"

I was perplexed at this response. I answered that I simply was curious. Abraham answered that she was lost during a flight and "the evidence of her disappearance was rapidly diminishing." As a side note, I believe this information totally fits in to the theory that TIGHAR has researched. I intuitively know TIGHAR's theory[4] is correct. This session ended with my being somewhat frustrated.

Around this time, due to her immense popularity, Esther stopped doing private readings. I was on a quest to find out more about my American lifetimes.

I had always felt the answers one needed would be found deep in oneself. My work with Jonathan and Larry seemed to confirm that. On the other hand, having an open mind was something that I thought to be a positive attribute, so I began another side quest to find people who could help me uncover some of the details of my past lives. I asked many of my contacts and used some of my own resources to find another medium or psychic who would be able to give specific answers. There was something driving me to find these answers that I didn't fully understand.

About one year later I had another session with a local woman who was a fairly-well-thought-of medium in the Chicago area. During that session she told me about several past lives. She referenced the American Revolution lifetime in details that fit with what little Abraham had told me. She made no mention of a Twentieth Century lifetime.

I decided to do one more session with her a few weeks later. This time I specifically asked if I had a connection with Amelia Earhart. This opened something up. She said that I was Amelia's husband, but I was more like a business partner.

All of a sudden she started channeling Amelia! Amelia told me that she was a little disappointed in my current lifetime, that she had expected bigger things of me. I asked Amelia if she could tell me who I was in the writer lifetime. She replied, "You'll know when you find the book with the rose on it." She also mentioned that I "should have taken better care of Sharron."

At this point the medium broke off contact with Amelia. She later told me that in her many decades of doing readings nothing like that had ever happened to her. "She must have really wanted to talk with you," the medium said. "I normally never desire to channel anyone other than the Ascended Masters. This is why I broke off contact." She also mentioned that Amelia had not reincarnated yet after that lifetime as she had work to do on the other side.

I was stunned. The medium told me I was Amelia's husband; however, Amelia refused to confirm this in so many words. Keep in mind that although I did mention Amelia by name, this was the first instance the medium knew about it. She would have had to have had intimate knowledge of Earhart's life to say what she did. Also, I never knew any of the details about Amelia, other than she was lost in 1937. I had never heard anything about her husband. I didn't even know she was married.

Over the next year I had sessions with two different psychics and one hypnotic regression. The first psychic told me that I did have a life in the first half of the 20th century. She could not give a specific name, however she said that I was a soldier during World War I and that I "lost someone very dear" to me, a loss that was still haunting me in this life. She also mentioned a Revolutionary War lifetime of note.

By this time I just started to look in to some of the details about Amelia's husband. I found out that he was a well-known writer, George Palmer Putnam (born 1887, died 1950). While thinking about this it made some sense. From my grade school days, I was fascinated by Amelia, and Putnam was her husband and a writer.

The fact that he died in 1950 also fit in with my feelings of "coming back too soon." While I don't know much about why people incarnate and when, I do know that if one has/had a trying life, I believe it can take time to assimilate things and learn from them on the other side. It was almost exactly seven years to the day that I reincarnated -- if I were indeed Putnam.

We can go into the facts about there being no time or space, quantum physics etc; to me this still fits. The one item that doesn't seem to fit, at least at this point, is the birth year. If what the psychic told me about WW I is true, Putnam would have been thirty when we became involved in the war. *A little old for this, although still possible*, I thought. More research would be needed.

I called up a psychic, whom I had not previously met. At this point, I thought I might be an incarnation of Putnam, but didn't know much about him. I was trying to corroborate facts to make me really believe I was indeed the reincarnation of the husband of the lost aviatrix.

This new psychic did her work and then told me that in my past life, which she didn't know anything about -- the whos or whats -- she sees, in her vision, lots of B-29 bombers. She described her vision to me as, "The sky is black with them." She told me that the reason she knew they were B-29s was the fact that her dad flew them in the war and he still had a strong attachment to them. B-29 models were everywhere around the house where she grew up and she had done a lot of research about them.

Keep in mind, she is seeing/imagining this, and she is trying to convey to me in the best way she can what she is seeing, sensing, and interpreting. (I have had literally thousands of these "visions" while doing session work for people, as well during as my own meditations, and I make the best sense out of them I can and try and convey the "knowing" that I have about them.)

What she did for me was to convey that, for one thing, this previous life of mine was involved with a *really big* B-29 raid based in China, bombers she could identify specifically. For another, she knew the raid was to bomb Japan. (This second "knowing" would have been a given for any student of WW II, of course, but she was relating a vision; no detail is too small.)

Putnam, it turns out, was a Major in China and was a key player in two big Army Air Corps B-29 raids against Japan, before the Marines took the islands that provided better bases.

The third thing she mentioned, though, was that I was "involved with" a Chinese woman she thought may have contributed to my death. (Interestingly, Putnam's first wife recounts in her book that he died of trichinosis which he likely picked up while stationed in China. Many American men became ill from the food there.)

She also mentioned a strong impression from the life around the time of the American Revolution. She saw me having to do with the signing of
important documents. She thought it may have been the Declaration of Independence! The Universe definitely works in mysterious ways. I managed to find the perfect psychic for this reading. Obvious to me: the Universe wants me to pursue this.

Since my work with Larry I had felt that it is better to not know anything about my clients. I felt it was not good to have any knowledge about anything related to them. I have since changed this view, as the confidence in my abilities is strong. Also, the fact that I have done so many readings and healings, I have found that it doesn't influence what I "get." Regarding my own reading, I was much more skeptical then than I am now regarding others' abilities and integrity. With all these readings' revolving around my search for past lives, I gave virtually no information about what I knew unless noted.

The next information I received was from hypnotic regression. This was the first time I had been regressed although I had seen several regressions performed on others. What I experienced with this was interesting. It was much like the information I would get when Larry and I worked.

I was in an altered state but conscious. The mind could still intervene and throw in a monkey wrench. However, I had long since learned that this was somewhat normal and knew how to dismiss it.

During the regression I confirmed that I was Putnam. I had a clear vision of walking to school one day. I could still see it. The hypnotist then asked me what I died of. I was taken aback. I was confused. *I didn't know what I died of.* Perhaps it was cancer, but I was perplexed that I didn't know. My mind told me I should know but I didn't. The hypnotist then directed me: "Go to the moment of your death…" I then had a strong vision, and even though the vision happened over twenty years ago, I saw it clearly: a hospital room, with a window straight ahead; the bed was to the right. There was an old-fashioned steam radiator under the window. I was lying in the bed and there was a woman between the far wall and the bed, next to me. As I came out of the regression I was unsure of the validity of the experience. I needed to do more research on Putnam with all this new information.

The internet was still pretty new, but I learned how use it to do research. Unfortunately, online information on Putnam was pretty scarce. I decided to go to the library; I wasn't sure what was available on him, but I wanted answers.

It had been many years since I had gone to the library. I was shocked that they didn't have card catalogs anymore! I found much information in *The New York Times*, including an article revealing that Major G. Putnam was an intelligence officer, stationed in China during WWII. The article went on to say that he was involved with the "biggest B29 raid on Japan to date." *Wow, the psychic said he was stationed in China and about the B29's. This was amazing! So, he would have been well into his fifties at this time. Could it be possible that he was in WWI also?*

Further research revealed that Putnam was indeed a lieutenant during WWI. He was involved with the family business, a publishing firm, Putnam and Sons, and died of uremic poisoning.

Also, it said that Putnam was Earhart's promoter, and more like a business partner than a husband, confirming what the medium had told me.

There is some debate on this point. However, the first medium picked up on something, as she never could have known anything of this sort. Through further research I found many fascinating similarities to my present life as well as much corroborating information that the psychics had given me.

Several years later I did a session with Kevin Reyerson on the recommendation of my highly respected friend, Dr. Norm Shealy. Reyerson confirmed that I was indeed Putnam and also one John Mathews. He didn't tell me much about Mathews except that he was involved in the family business and lawyer. He also stated that there was a portrait that existed of Mathews.

Reyerson told me that Amelia had incarnated in the last ten to fifteen years or so, which fits into the timeframe and information the medium had given me, that Amelia had not incarnated yet, in the reading some fifteen years earlier. He also said he believed that "Amelia" would become a student of mine in this lifetime. I subsequently found out that

Mathews was a signer of the Articles of Confederation and thirty-third governor of South Carolina. (I found a portrait on Ancestors.com years later.)

Also, I found out that Dorothy Binney, Putnam's first of four wives (Amelia was his second), had written an extensive diary. In the book, <u>Whistled Like a Bird</u>, Putnam's daughter, Sally Putnam Chapman (with co-author Stephanie Mansfield) cites excerpts from Binney's diary.

One other fascinating tidbit was that Putnam requested an autopsy upon his death, since neither he nor his doctors knew why his health was declining. It turns out he died of trichinosis, a parasite he must have picked up from eating diseased pork while stationed in China. *Could the woman mentioned by the one psychic have been the one who prepared the pork causing his death?* Another interesting fact is that the symptoms of trichinosis are quite similar to fibromyalgia!

Putnam died in a hospital in Trona, California, another confirmation of my regression. I highly recommend <u>Whistled Like a Bird</u>, as it is a fascinating story!

Reyerson, who is the most accurate intuitive I have encountered in terms of minute details, told me of several other lifetimes of note. Many details that he has given to clients have been later verified. I have no doubt of his incredible gifts. As mentioned, he cleared up the mystery of the Revolutionary War period, and also mentioned that prior to the Putnam life I had been a half Native American, half Scotch, who knew Custer and had served in several campaigns with him. (I died in battle in that lifetime, although not at the Little Big Horn.) Like my fascination with Amelia I have had a lifetime fascination with Custer, although the more I learned of him the less I liked him and his actions. I believe that I was half Shoshone and that I loved their land as much as I love my farm. I can see why I love the Rockies so much!

The lifetime immediately before that one was interesting. I was a man living in Scotland who became a medical doctor. I attended the University of Edinbrough. I eventually contracted tuberculosis (then called consumption) and died of that illness. I was on a quest to find a cure for TB, not so much for myself but to alleviate people's suffering. My intuition tells me that I crossed paths with a man named John Elliotson.

Elliotson was a prior life of Dr. Norm Shealy's. Before this lifetime, I was John Mathews, mentioned earlier. It seems that I have died young in this procession of lifetimes as well as reincarnating fairly quickly, usually in under ten years.

One last lifetime of note that Reyerson mentioned was that I was a son of Ramses II. His reign was perhaps the most significant in Egyptian history. According to Reyerson, I was in charge of the lunar calendar. This is akin to the medicine man or religious leader during the reign of Ramses. Reyerson told a friend of mine that she is the incarnation of Hatshepsup, another truly notable figure in Egyptian history. I have many memories of being in Egypt and Atlantis. No doubt that my friend and I are from the same soul group.

In this life, Norm also introduced me to Walter Semkiw. Semkiw is a physician, and who, like Norm, is a brilliant man. He quit his practice and wrote the book, <u>Return of the Revolutionaries: The Case for Reincarnation and Soul Groups Reunited</u>. I often think to myself that in many cases it takes a brilliant mind to grasp what may seem absurd to the majority. Upon talking with Semkiw I found out that as a youngster he spent his summers about 20 minutes from my farm. He also said he wanted to put my story of the Putnam life on his website, although to date nothing has appeared on it. Again, I felt a connection to Semkiw which, as I unfold spiritually, I find is happening more and more.

I recommend going to Reincarnation Research.com to find out more about Semkiw's work.

What does it all mean? Something had pressed me to find answers. Throughout my life whenever I have had a strong desire, I feel like something is pushing me. I haven't had this happen many times, but it has happened with my spiritual search several times, with purchasing my farm, and with golf. Looking back, these have been my greatest transformative undertakings.

One thing I do know is that in each instant I had to let go of a strong attachment. My golf was the most straightforward example of this. My drive to become "great" was so strong and it was fueled by a negative emotion. I have learned much about the yin and yang of things. Everything lies on a continuum. More about this later.

I was pushed to find out more about my past lives. Upon my own inner work, I now know that it was because I had carried many energies with me throughout many incarnations. My work with Parker and especially with Larry emphasized this. As I discovered common threads and patterns, I was more easily able to let them go in this lifetime. I believe, and have told many of my clients, that past lives don't need to be taken literally. They could sometimes be an analogy, and I believe sometimes they are. While talking with Norm Shealy one day, he said basically the same thing.

Some things I have in common with some of my previous lives is that we (I) worked for a family business and were in positions of relative power and wealth. Putnum mentioned in his autobiography that he had always wanted to live in the mountains – my own dream. He, like me, invested in a large parcel of land and built a large house. His house, like mine, had a massive main room fireplace. He also had an extensive art collection that included many examples of Rockwell Kent's work.

Kent's work is described: *Often cited as an early American Modernist, Kent's work focuses on the otherworldly beauty of nature, influenced by Transcendentalism and the mysticism of writers such as Henry David Thoreau and Ralph Waldo Emerson*[5].

My connection to Jean Paul Avisse is eerily similar:

Throughout the next several years I had many breakthroughs pertaining to old patterns. If it would not have been for my past life work I am not sure I could have found some of this stuck energy, let alone release it. Remember the woman and the Reiki masters? When I asked about her father, she was able to let go of the trapped crystallized energy in an instant. She had had that energy during much of that original and subsequent lives.

In this instance, she didn't need to go back into previous lives to release it, as the story I told her was enough. Perhaps, in the future, other aspects or frequencies of this energy may show up and it may help her to trace the threads back.

I believe that my current lifetime's goal is to release many old patterns while helping others heal in the process. My soul, spirit, higher self, or whatever you want to call it chose the manner to accomplish this. From looking back on some of the masters who attained Freedom, I believe that in incarnations prior to the ones in which they became Free, they did work much like this. Hence, many of the ancient mystery schools existed to help with this process of release.

As an interesting aside, through my research and subsequent meditations on my Putnam life, I gained a lot of insight on that man, and his personality/ego that is not what history generally portrays him as. History paints him as a very intelligent, driven, harsh and uncaring man. He would do anything to further his goals and wanted attention. The movie *Amelia* portrays Putnam in this manner and I believe it was derived from Doris Rich's book on Amelia. Also, many contemporaries of Putnam did not really understand the man.

In Sally Putnam Chapman's book, <u>Whistled Like A Bird</u>, those close to him described him thus: "George Palmer Putnam was eulogized as a generous, if somewhat difficult man by his friends and family. An intelligent intellectual, he was often misunderstood by those who sought his approval and envied his success."

As Robert Lee recalled, "GPP is remembered more for his eccentricities than his virtues. His fame is clouded by the clout of his candor. He was a genius at befriending large people and offending small ones. Yet, as in our case, he was our staunch friend because of a shared admiration. He dismissed stupidity. He was no celebrity-chaser. One of his best friends was a forest ranger at Whitney Portal named Shorty…"

Also, the book mentioned his need to be in the mountains and have seclusion. The book talked of his wanting to hike and push his body physically. I am, in my current personality, much the same. By understanding on a deep level the personality of Putnam, I can more fully understand my true
nature which is an undying part of the Divine Spark.

On a different note, one day I was perusing a magazine called *The Monthly Aspectarian*. This was a local Chicago-based metaphysical magazine. It is where I first heard of Sharon Wendt. On this month's cover was a surrealistic painting. I longed to know more about this piece of art. The picture was done by a French artist whose name is Jean Paul Avisse. The painting in question was of a beautiful girl holding a violin, with a surreal background. I had been to this spot, or one very much like the one in the painting. I had traveled there often in my meditations. I found a gentleman named Louis Schutz was the only person in the world licensed to sell Avisse's works. Louis had an art gallery in Skokie, Illinois, not far from my childhood home.

I contacted Louis and made an appointment to come to his gallery. When I got there he had approximately eight original Avisse paintings hanging in a room. As I entered the room I felt like I was entering a holy church. Seeing, feeling, and remembering these scenes was itself surreal. The energy in this room was intense! I learned from Louis that Avisse paints like the old masters, using plywood instead of canvas and taking sometimes over a year to complete a painting. Over the next several years I bought two giclees and one original painting which also graced the cover of *The Aspectarian*.

I found Louis to be unusually open, friendly, and gracious. While visiting his gallery on one occasion, I asked him what his favorite Avisse piece was. He replied, "Oh, I have that in a private area upstairs and will probably never sell it as I love it so much." He let me see it.

It was a somewhat simpler painting than Avisse's usual, although one would never say any of Avisse's works were "usual!" This painting was of a young woman wearing a hooded robe with her hands folded in prayer. She had a gaze that was somewhat reminiscent of the Mona Lisa. It was an absolutely beautiful painting and I could see why Louis liked it so much.

Months later, around Christmas time, I entered my office at work and saw a copy of that painting sitting there next to my desk. Upon inquiry I learned that Louis gave it to me as a gift. I called him to thank him and to ask why. He simply replied that he loved it so much he thought I would appreciate it, which I did.

On another occasion while talking to my wife, he learned that we traveled to visit our son in North Carolina where he was attending college. He told her, "Seeing as you sold your dealership, and you will probably have items to move back and forth, I will let you use my big old station wagon to go out there. Just call me any time!" Louis is just that sort of guy. He later closed his gallery and I have lost track of him, although our paths did cross about five years ago. Again, I intuit we have met in a previous life/lives.

While working with Parker and Larry, I learned that one could create instantly in the

Astral by thought. I experimented with this quite a bit over the years and found that I was drawn to create a place in the high Himalayas whereby I could meditate in a high-energy environment with the Ascended Masters. Many of these places are almost identical to what Avisse paints. I have never met Avisse but feel surely that he paints from his inner experiences which are similar to mine.

Again, I find that I am drawn to many people who are from my soul group. Many of these people have shared past lives with me. As an aside, I believe soul groups are from a similar or close spark of the Divine.

I think of soul groups as a patchwork quilt of sorts, one large quilt made up of many different patches. The quilt would be analogous to the One. The patches would be the soul groups. When you encounter people with whom you resonate or are attracted to, it is probably that you are from that particular patch or group. The farther one patch is from another, still being part of the quilt, the more one would tend not to resonate with that person/group of people. I believe certain countries have a large part of their populations comprised of the same soul group, as well as families etc. I could talk a lot more about this but will save it for a future time.

[4] www.tighar.org.
[5] www.artnet.com

Chapter 7: Bringing in the New Millennium

In late 1999, I was enthused at the progress I had made in my life. I felt called to start working on my physical health. I had been so focused on helping others that I neglected my own body. I spent the previous ten years immersed in spiritual practice to become clearer. I thought this would transfer down into the physical body.

For the most part it didn't. Many of my energy bodies had become much clearer. My emotions and mental body had changed dramatically, however my physical remained racked with the pain of fibromyalgia. It wasn't until the late 1990s that I learned what a lot of my pain was. A rheumatologist confirmed a diagnosis of FMS after a chiropractor friend told me what it was. I decided to spend two weeks at the Myofacial Pain Center in Sedona, Arizona.

I knew Sedona well, as Parker had many of his seminars there. My first visit there was in the early 1970s with my parents. I remember that my mom loved it. She loved the energy and felt wonderful there. In the early '70s it was nothing like it is today. It was not really known as a metaphysical hotspot, although it was known for its scenic beauty. I loved the energy there also. I took my wife and young children there in the mid '90s. We stayed at a resort in Boynton Canyon. This canyon was said to have a lot of energy like many spots around Sedona.

One day we decided to take a walk up the canyon. My wife had a double stroller as our kids were approximately two and four years old. Even though it was rocky, there was a path, so we were able to negotiate it, at least for a while, with the stroller. Up in the hills we saw Native American ruins and a path to them. I asked my wife if she would mind waiting for a while below with the kids as I would like to hike up to it. We were used to hiking in the mountains so it didn't seem like a big deal to me.

I worked my way up the path and about halfway up I reached a large smooth rock. This was an unmistakable landmark if you were familiar with this trail. I started up the smooth surface of the rock when I couldn't go any farther. I felt a strong sense of dread. I thought it must just be me. I decided to sit down and wait a few minutes. I tried to ascend again but something stopped me. I tried three or four more times, and every time the same thing happened. I couldn't figure it out. I decided to go down and told my wife what had happened.

She was a seasoned hiker and said, "Wait a minute. I'll go up there and see what's going on." She ascended and I waited there with the kids. About a half hour later she came down and told me she felt the same thing. She couldn't go on. As the kids were getting cranky and it was late we decided to go back to our room.

The next day arrived and I was eager to go to the ruins. Now it was a matter of principle. My wife and kids stayed back at the resort to have some fun and I went back to the path. I got back up to the point where I had stopped before and the same thing happened. I tried several more times, same thing.

This day there happened to be many hikers in the canyon. As I sat at the base of the smooth rock, people would come and go up to the ruins without batting an eye. This was starting to get me angry! I unsuccessfully tried to go past that point for a couple of hours and I couldn't do it. I sat there and meditated and didn't get any answers.

The next day was our last at the resort. We needed to drive back to Phoenix that afternoon. I told my wife "One last time!" I reached that spot and *bang*, something stopped me. An intense wave of dread came over me. I said to myself, *If I die in the attempt, I'm doing it!* I virtually ran up that smooth rock as if I had been chased by a bear. I made it to the ruins and meditated there for about an hour. Coming down was no problem. I never did get any answers myself, but this isn't the end of the story.

About one year later, an employee of mine that had been with me for many years told me he was leaving for vacation the next day. As we talked he mentioned that he, his wife, and a group of their friends were going to Sedona. He told me that he really didn't want to go there, but his wife was into meditation and energy work and they wanted to visit there.

I had never known his wife had those interests before. I told him about Boynton Canyon. I said that if they made it there to go to the

Indian ruins as they were very neat and had a special energy.

He didn't seem impressed, as I could tell he thought metaphysics was just mumbo jumbo. I told him to tell his wife. I didn't mention my experience there as I was curious what might happen.

A couple of weeks later he came back to work, and first thing, he came into my office. He told me that they did in fact visit Boynton Canyon and went up to that spot where there was a large smooth rock. His group, which consisted of himself, his wife and two other couples all tried to go up to the ruins and were stopped as they tried to go up the smooth rock. Just like my wife and I, they attempted it several times and couldn't do it.

As they were standing at the rock, a couple of Native Americans were coming down from the ruins. My employee asked them what they were doing up there as they were carrying a bunch of stuff down the hill from the ruins. They replied that there had just been a ceremony held at the ruins and they were leaving. The ruins, he said, were sacred. My friend related to them how they felt an intense energy at this spot that wouldn't let them proceed. The Native American replied, "This is to be expected. We (the Native Americans) placed a curse on this spot to keep trespassers out. Also, in a past life you were a cavalry officer who committed many crimes against us."

My employee related that the Native American seemed to have no animosity towards him or his group. He seemed rather matter of fact about it. It is interesting that although I did feel intense dread, I didn't understand why I was feeling it. Also, it is interesting that in my past life searching I was a half Shoshone / half Scottish cavalry scout. Did this energy force field have something to do with the fact that we were both in the cavalry in previous lifetimes?

So now it was fall of 1999, and I was in back in Sedona. I was put through many intense therapies for the next two weeks. I had many physical releases. I felt that almost all of the work I had done up to that point had neglected the physical body. Now I was experiencing physical release and I was able to feel the energy and emotions associated with them. As I went home after those two weeks, I actually looked different. I was told to continue a vigorous stretching routine they had given me.

As with any instruction, I tend to follow it to the letter. I have incredible will power. Through the years, dealing with as much pain as I have, I can compartmentalize many facets of my life. I think of myself somewhat as Spock in the original *Star Trek* series. I can shut pain out, emotions, or pretty much anything I want. I can eat or not eat. I have tried many diets and can stick with anything I set my mind to.

So, when I got back home, I was stretching several times a day per their instructions. One of the stretches was to really work my neck. As I continued this, after a couple of weeks I noticed some pain in my left ear. It became extremely intense, for only a second or two, and then would subside. After a few days of this I was brushing my teeth before bed and I couldn't hold water in my mouth to rinse. I noticed the left side of my face was numb. I told my wife and she told me to go to the emergency room. I decided to wait until morning. By then, my left face was pretty much incapacitated. I went to the emergency room and waited almost four hours to finally see a doctor. They said I had Bell's palsy and there wasn't much they could do for me. I asked if it could be anything else and they pretty much ruled out a stroke. The only other thing would be something called Ramsey Hunt. If it was that, they said, I would be in such severe pain that I wouldn't be able to stand it.

Several days later, I developed blisters on my left ear. I called a doctor the emergency room had set me up with as a follow-up doctor.

She said, "Oh, you have Ramsey Hunt. It's too bad that they didn't put you on antiviral, as if you catch it early it can really help. Come in in a few days, and in the meantime go to see a neurologist." I should note that the left half of my face was totally paralyzed. I had to tape my eye shut so it wouldn't dry out, and I couldn't eat solid food.

I immediately called the neurologist they recommended. I told the receptionist that I needed to get in right away, etc. She literally laughed. She replied, "You can't just get in to see Dr. H! He is booked up for the next four weeks."

I replied, "What am I supposed to do?"

She said, "Well I will put you down in four weeks." I didn't know what to do so I just said ok.

Two days later, we had a severe snowstorm. I knew there would be cancellations, so I called the neurologist's office. Sure enough, I got in that day.

The doctor greeted me with, "Wow, the left side of your left face is pretty much gone!" Great opening line to tell a patient! After he examined me I asked him what the chances were that I might regain mobility. Just like his receptionist, he literally laughed. As he did he said, "Due to the severity of the paralysis, you probably won't get any better. But don't worry. We can insert a weight in to your eyelid so you will be able to close it."

I was devastated. I decided to work hours every day and run energy to the nerves. The emergency room visit was on December 1st, 1999. Three weeks later, I still had no movement in that part of my face. My lip was raw from biting it as it hung under my teeth. I had to have my eye taped shut most of the time.

At a little over three weeks, I felt a slight feeling on that side. Over the next six months, I continually worked my muscles and sent energy. I regained about 80% movement, although I still have a lot of numbness in my eyelid, and my smile, which used to be captivating, is now somewhat lopsided. Still, I feel fortunate that I recovered as much as I did. Interestingly, that first tinge of feeling came to me on my forty-third birthday.

This event marked another Dark Night of the Soul for me. It was a night that lasted about ten years. While there was a lot of good in this time, my spiritual search took a confusing turn. After falling flat with my dream of creating a network of healers came to an end, and the family business started to decline due to changing tastes and demographics, I lost direction. I felt betrayed, like I had felt when I was a youngster. *How could God allow things to fall flat when I was so dedicated?* I decided to stop meditating and concentrate on the material life. In 2001, my dad fell ill. Again, uncaring and what I believe to be incompetent doctors misdiagnosed a serious condition.

My dad died of glyoblastoma in June 2002. This was a devastating blow to me. My life-long friend, the only person on the planet that had an inkling of what I went through, was now gone. Also, I had lost my faith. After my dad passed, the energy that held the family business really nosedived. What had been a negative trend was now enhanced by a lack of my dad's positive energy.

In the fall of 2002, we sold our body shop business, which, when we built it in 1995, was one of the largest in the Midwest. We maintained ownership of the building. We sold to one of the finest men I have known in the business world, Roger D'Orazio. I had run this part of our business the previous three years.

This move turned out to be extremely positive for us. Several years later Roger got out of the business. We have been fortunate to have had excellent tenants in the building since.

In 2004 I became involved with Sufism. I had been looking for something to give me some direction. In a roundabout way, Jonathan Parker had a hand in this chapter of my life. I remember his talking about energy healers and the name Robert Jaffe had come up. Parker heard many good things about him and the name stuck in my head for many years.

I was looking on line at something and the name Jaffe again came up. He had had an epiphany and converted to Islam. Jaffe was a medical doctor and was diagnosed with a terminal heart condition. He met Sidi al Jamal and was cured by him. He was now one of the heads of the University of Sufism based in Napa Valley, California.

Chapter 8: Sufi Path: the 180-degree Continuum

2004 marked my introduction into Sufism. I had studied aspects of it in my metaphysical studies, however I didn't know much about it. During 2004 I took some telecourses and I happened to meet Sandy Crowe in that first teleclass. I mentioned her in the acknowledgments. It turns out she didn't like me at all! Once we met, that changed, and have been friends ever since.

In 2005, I enrolled in their formal school. It consisted of four one-week classes every year. The complete "basic" course would last three years. It felt foreign to me, and very rigid. It reminded me of my Catholic years, only in many ways it was more stringent.

During the first class I felt isolated, since most of my class consisted of people who were already familiar with this path; by the end of that first week, there were only three people who did not have Sufi names.

In this sect, Sidi Mohammad Al Jamal, who was the imam at The Dome of the Rock in Jerusalem, was our guide or leader. "Sidi" means "teacher" in Arabic. He was the one who would give us our Sufi names. The name was usually a quality of Allah or God. In Islam, God is called Allah; the feminine aspect of Allah is Laila.

By that last day of my first class I vowed to never give in and get a Sufi name! I still carried a lot of resistance against being told what to do. Throughout that first week I began hearing stories of Sidi, as they called our leader. Many of the stories related people's experiences of miracles performed by Sidi.

Another aspect I didn't like was that all the men except a few wore hats. These hats were known as kufis. Women were also expected to cover their heads. I have disliked hats from my early days golfing, and I didn't want to give in. I had always been a non-conformist.

At lunch the last day of that first class, I sat next to one of the teachers. She was a trained psychologist with respectable credentials. We talked of Sidi. I asked many questions about him and I became intrigued with the man. *Could this be the guru or guide I had hoped for?* Also, somehow we got on the subject of

Eugene Gendlin, who wrote a book on psychology which was was one of the bases of Larry's work. She had actually had lunch with Gendlin years earlier.

She gave me Sidi's phone number in Jerusalem and what times he was available to talk. Keep in mind, Sidi was the imam at the Dome of the Rock. This is, I believe, the third most holy mosque in Islam and maybe the most famous. Sidi had millions of followers. He was also said to be an *Insan al Kamal*, or perfected being. They only supposedly incarnate every several hundred years. He was also directly related to the prophet Mohammad, may peace and blessings be upon him.

When I returned home I had a lot to think about. I started to read one of Sidi's books which didn't make much sense to me. I was still unsure about all this and I was in the midst of a spiritual as well as life crisis. I was questioning everything and wasn't sure about anything. The '90s were my breakout years and I had gained so much confidence. Now I was in a quandary.

After the second class I was, I think, the only person in the class to not have a Sufi name. I decided to call Sidi up and receive a name. I couldn't understand him as he didn't speak English well and had a very thick accent.

I don't think he understood me and I wasn't sure of anything he said. I think I made out that my name was Abdullah, although for all I knew I may have ordered a pepperoni pizza from some guy in Jerusalem. Boy, the delivery charges would be crazy!

I wound up completing the three years of school as well as an additional two to obtain a Master's degree in Sufi Spiritual Ministry.

My daughter, who was in high school at the time, wanted to attend based on what I had told her about Sidi. She completed the first two years, being one year behind me. She was a joy to have with me as we learned much about Sufism.

At Sufi school I met Luis Torolla, whom I have mentioned in the acknowledgments. It turns out that he moved from Argentina to study Kriya Yoga at Self Realization in Los Angeles. At that point he didn't even speak English. So not only do we have the Kriya connection, we also seem to have similar views on our spiritual path. The move to America was a huge leap of faith for him. We have remained good friends ever since. I feel a past life connection here.

I will give a brief summary of some of what I experienced in Sufi school. (The entire experience would require another book.) My daughter and I became close with Sidi. He showed much love for us. It was so noticeable that many people over the years commented on it. He would literally light up when he saw me or my daughter. I was told by Sidi's aide that he would often make special prayers specifically for us, which was unusual for him to do.

During the period from 2005-2010 I spent approximately three months per year away on Sufi excursions. These included classes and *Zawiyahs*, or retreats. During one of these Zawiyas, Sidi was sitting on a porch and called out "Abdullah, Come here!" Somewhat perplexed, as Sidi did not usually do this, I complied.

Sidi gave me a bear hug and said "Abdullah, I LOVE you." I was stunned but really felt honored that he would take the time to do this for me. I had never seen him do this for anyone. I was able to spend one-on-one time with Sidi.

One of the highlights of my Sufi experience was to do many *Dikkars*. I won't go into all of the details here but it involved an escalating counterclockwise flow of energy culminating in an ecstatic tracelike state. It may be

considered similar to, but not exactly like the whirling Dervishes:
Maybe a hundred people would be in a circle and a leader, or several leaders would direct the energy, and I learned how to lead them during my Master's degree class.

Sidi would sometimes have one of the beloveds, or disciples channel Mother Mary or Archangel Gabriel. He would have a group of about ten people sit around him. He would then take the channel's hand and write sacred Arabic script on their hand and arm. The person would be overshadowed by whatever spirit was called, and enter a trancelike state. I was right next to Sidi and the channel one time, and the energy was palpable.

Another instance: I was with Sidi during some sort of special prayer. He took both my hands in his. He was going to perform something that I cannot now recall; he didn't have some item that he needed, so he sent a runner to get it. We sat together for about ten minutes as he held both my hands in a steely grip. It was an amazing experience as he related some stories about his grandfather and sent me incredible loving energy.

Sidi was a small man but built like a fireplug. His hands were huge. In his youth, he must have been physically very powerful. By the time I met him he was well into his seventies and somewhat frail. There is a recording of him from the late 1950s where he sang channeled poetry for several hours while on Hajj. It was said that there were hundreds who gathered around as he channeled and sang what he was getting from Allah. They all knew they were in the presence of a great sage.

Another incident was told me by several people, one of whom said he actually witnessed it: One day in Jerusalem, Israeli soldiers opened fire on some children around the Dome of the Rock. Sidi, it is said, ran and shielded one of the children with his body. An Israeli soldier later came forward and said that he was a trained sniper and had shot Sidi several times. He said that he knew he had hit Sidi multiple times. After the incident, he went to Sidi to ask forgiveness. Sidi forgave him on the spot and the Israeli soldier immediately became a disciple of Sidi's. This witness said Sidi's *jalaba*, or cloak, had several bullet holes in it that he personally saw. Sidi was untouched!

Another Sidi story that I find amazing was told me by the person that it happened to. This woman was in my class and is a beautiful soul. Every year she and a group of her friends would take a trip. This year they decided to go to Thailand. The first night there she had a vivid dream in which Sidi came to her and said, "You must leave as quickly as possible. Go back home." She woke after the dream and thought, *What an odd dream*. The next night she had another dream where Sidi said, "You must leave here tomorrow!" Upon awakening, she became alarmed. Still, she took no action. The next night Sidi came to her during sleep and said, "This is your last chance. Please leave!" She finally heeded this warning, took a flight out, and the next day the big Tsunami hit, wiping out the resort where she had been staying. The next time she saw Sidi she thanked him for his warning and he replied, "But why did it take three warnings for you to listen to me?"

There was a group in Chicago that used to host Sidi when he was in town. (He often made quick tours around the country to visit beloveds.) I would occasionally go to meetings this group would hold. I got to know one gentleman pretty well and he told me that one day while Sidi was giving a talk in his home the doorbell rang. It was the UPS man.

One of the men opened the door and received a package. Sidi yelled out in a loud voice, "Bring this man in!" The host asked the UPS driver to come inside and Sidi quickly rushed up to greet him. "Welcome beloved," Sidi said. "Why has it taken you so long to come to me?" The UPS man ran for the hills, totally confused by this greeting!

Another time it was related to me that one of the people from the Chicago group was in a circle of about fifteen people where Sidi was leading prayers. Most people had their eyes closed as the energy would intensify while Sidi prayed, putting people in an ecstatic state. He told me that he wanted to see what was going on when Sidi prayed like this.

He kept his attention on Sidi, who was sitting a couple of places away. He swore Sidi levitated a good ten inches off the ground! From my experiences with Kriya yoga I know this to be a phenomenon occasionally witnessed with adepts.

It was at about this time that I took the Muslim promise from Sidi. I frequently led the Muslim prayer in front of groups numbering about a hundred people. One has to sing the prayers in Arabic and remember all of the "rules," praying, standing, bowing, etc. If the leader of the prayer does something incorrectly and realizes it, then the prayer is void and had to be repeated, I believe from the beginning. I was deathly afraid of singing in public, let alone having that responsibility on me. I had learned Arabic phonetically, and was amazed at how well the prayers would flow when I sang them.

One of the interesting things about Islam is that they believe that Allah has certain qualities, and this is where your Muslim name usually comes in. A quality like Salaam means peace. Although no one specifically taught me this, I believe every quality of God, or really anything has a 180-degree continuum, like the Yin and Yang, male and female, etc. I knew several people to whom Sidi gave the name of Salaam. I noticed, as with all the names he gave, it totally described the person in question. People named Salaam tended to be calm indeed. However, much of their life struggle revolves around conflict. I believed that the name was a clue on what they needed to work on. I believe Salaam's life mission, in part, is to lose their attachments and have peace.

An example might be someone who is bipolar. Manic depressives, as they used to be called, can be upbeat and calm one minute, then depressed, angry and short-tempered in the next. I am not saying that this is always the case with bipolar disorder, but it illustrates my point.

The name Sidi gave me was *Abdullah*. This is not a specific quality of God but means *slave of God*, and in our school was the dreaded name to be given, as it was usually given to people that were selfless individuals that had to clean up all the other people's messes! Uncannily, it seemed an accurate description.

I soon began to teach in front of groups of people. For my Master's Practicum I did a book of channeled poetry entitled "An Oasis of Hope." During this master's program I started teaching totally without a plan or notes. Everything I did was *ad lib*. I found my teachings had taken on a totally new energy. For one of my final tests for my Master's, I was given two short lines from a *sura* (prayer). I was given these lines cold and told to talk on them for twenty minutes. I had no problem doing this -- what I received and then spoke was totally channeled. I could have talked for hours on only two lines!

I was given a directive, in part by Sidi, that when I taught, I was to teach only from Sidi's books. I was told that one of the leaders of the Chicago group was not impressed by my teaching, that I was not "pure" enough in what I taught, even though I was told that my classes had the highest attendance of any teacher's in that group. I really wanted to make a difference there, and I was dismayed at this criticism of my efforts.

As with most organized groups, I felt there was a tremendous amount of infighting and jealousy. As mentioned earlier, there was a spiritual elitism and closed-mindedness to things that didn't conform to "the rules."

As with Parker, Larry, and many other disciplines, I reached a point where I felt change was needed. Mainly, I felt the Sufis in this sect were too rigid and they had told me that I needed to change my old ways of living in what would be considered the "astral" world.

During this time, I had lost almost all my second sight and much of what I had learned previously had become cloudy. Part of it was as a directive by the Sufi "teachers" that I needed to change, and part was confusion about what was "right."

I completely changed the way in which I healed. I was critiqued by Robert Jaffe himself and I was voted to be the "best healer" in our class of about forty, along with one other person, even though this type of healing didn't feel right to me.

In the summer of 2010, Sidi came to Chicago and I met with him in private. I told him that I had decided to quit the path. He started to cry. I loved Sidi and I knew he loved me, but I felt this was something I needed to do. After I quit, I felt tremendous guilt and was extremely sad. I felt cut off and alone. I was experiencing physical withdrawal symptoms!

I started reading about cults and how people become entrapped and stuck. Cult withdrawal symptoms were eerily similar to mine. I am not saying that this was a cult, however I had become attached to it. In many ways it acted as a sort of safety net for me, yet overall I feel my Sufi experience had a tremendous detrimental effect on me (that perceived negativity again). It took me well over a year to finally break free from the attachment.

I never saw him again.
Sidi passed away on November 11, 2015.

Chapter 9: End of My Dark Decade of the Soul

In 2010 I was heartbroken and had experienced a very difficult ten years. In late 1999, I suffered from Ramsey Hunt syndrome, and then I quit my spiritual path in 2000. I lost my dad in 2002. In 2006 we sold the family business, so I retired shortly before my fiftieth birthday. The Sufi experience, although positive in some aspects, was a real drain for me, due to the infighting and confusion among the members. I wasn't sure what to do next.

Several months after that last meeting with Sidi, I had a formal introduction to Dr. Norm Shealy, made by, of all people, one of the Sufi teachers I knew. I talked with Norm over the phone and decided to spend two weeks on retreat at Norm's Brindabella Farms. This is where his Holos Institute is located. My main goal was to have him help me manage my chronic fatigue and fibromyalgia.

I had known of Norm since the early '90s and was impressed by his credentials and work. I was also familiar with his work with Caroline Myss and had read many of her books. When I arrived at Brindabella, I was pleased to find out that he and his wife had moved from Wisconsin to Missouri in the late '80s. They had had a horse farm and moved it to Missouri at that time. Another synchronicity!

I met with Norm that first day and we talked for a couple of hours. It was conducted like a job interview. We sat outside his Missouri home on the patio. As I described my life experiences and spiritual quest he stood up at least half a dozen times and came over to me and shook my hand. It seems many of the things I had done and beliefs I had were in common with his. He gave me a lot of validation, which at that point in my life I sorely needed.

I spent the next two weeks getting intravenous "Meyer's Cocktails" (high doses of B vitamins, magnesium, and, in my case, vitamin C). Also, I was worked on by Dave Schulte.

Dave is an incredible highly intuitive body worker. I won't call him a "massage therapist," as he is a lot more than that. Dave would work on me at least a couple hours a day. I would then have Norm's assistant, Robert, lead me through various things like putting me on Norm's *rejuvamatrix* or crystal rooms to meditate in. Like me, Norm is really into crystals and music, as well as reading.

In fact, Holos Institute had tons of quartz crystals mixed into its foundation. There is one room where the entire floor, ceiling and walls are made of crystal.

In the '90s, when I began work with Larry, I started to be able to talk to crystals and found that they contained much energy that could be healing. I used crystals to aid in my healings as well as different colors or rays of light.

I spent time with Norm every day during those two weeks. I found him to be one of the most fascinating people I have ever met. Norm is a truly loving individual.

Another thing that impressed me with Norm was, on that first day, he mentioned The Urantia Book. He was the first person I had met who has not only read the whole book, over 2000 pages, but understood it. I had been a big fan of the book since early in my metaphysical quest, although in fairness I can't say that I understand much of the first half of it.

When it came time to leave Norm I was, for probably the first time in my life, pain free. The fatigue hadn't gotten any better, but the burning fibromyalgia pain was pretty much gone. Norm gave me a final interview to assess my progress. During my two weeks with Norm I believe he found me to be a fairly straight laced, somewhat shy person. Shortly after my arrival he started to call me Dean-Baby. I am not sure why he did this but I liked it. As I was leaving, I, in a serious tone, asked, "Norm, would you do me a very big favor?" Norm turned various serious and said, "It depends" I was thinking to myself, *He probably thinks I am going to ask him for some money*. (lol). I then asked, "Norm, can I call you Norm-Baby?"

With a big smile he replied, "Yes, but not in public!" Upon returning home, the pain came back, but never quite to the degree it had gotten to before Norm's. This point marked my finally coming out of my dark night of the soul.

Since leaving Norm's I have kept in touch with him and his assistant Robert. They are always accessible and gracious. Norm has done me several favors over the years for which I am extremely grateful. I truly value his friendship.

A couple of months later, I took Marla to see Dave, Norm's body worker in Missouri, as I was so impressed with him. I had been to dozens of body workers, massage therapists, and energy healers and had never encountered anyone as gifted as Dave. Norm told me that he too had been to, or seen many body workers, and Dave was the best.

Marla and I both had a great healing and relaxing time with Dave. On our way back home my brother called me to say that my mom was in the hospital, very sick. He wasn't sure she would make it. This was sudden; Marla and I rushed back.

My mom wound up recovering from that initial scare; however she was diagnosed with lung cancer. My mom was eighty-three at the time and had been complaining for the last few years of tiredness. She was still sharp mentally and physically active until this time.

I would visit her several times a week and my family used to like to take her out to lunch or dinner often. My kids really loved her, as she was a kind and gentle soul. Both my kids were in college at the time, but my son saw her a couple of months before she passed, as did my daughter about a week before.

It was very sad, although I am glad that I had spent time with her quite a bit since my dad had passed some nine years earlier.

Later that year, 2011, I started doing something called the Release Technique. It is an offshoot of the Sedona Method started by Lester Levinson. The Release Technique was started by one of Lester's students, Larry Crane.

Larry reminded me a lot of my dad. Both men had a huge heart but were tough as nails. I went to my first retreat with the technique in March of 2012. Here I met my dear friend Griselda. Since our initial meeting we worked together extensively and talk several times a week. I took an immediate liking to her, and she has been a great friend and resource for me ever since that first meeting. Our kids seem similar as well. We both have a son and daughter with similar personalities. Griselda and I also share similar childhoods.

That first retreat was excellent although for some, they didn't understand where Larry Crane was coming from. Because he was like my dad, I was perfectly comfortable with him. Also, during this retreat, Griselda's deceased mother came to me in the middle of class. This was a clear and a somewhat unusual thing to happen to me while not in meditation. I described the visit to Griselda, even down to what her mother was wearing and she said, "That was her. You gave a perfect description of a rather unusual coat she was wearing."

I went to all the Release Technique retreats for the next couple of years. At one of them I had a spiritual awakening. I won't be able to convey it in words as it was an experience to me. It also emphasizes that one never knows when something like this can occur. I had spent years with Sidi, a supposed "perfected individual," and never had anything like this occur.

Right then, I had the realization that I could choose to feel any particular way at any particular time. In the midst of chaos I could choose to panic or be at peace. Upon hearing "dreadful" news, I can choose to become upset or happy. *It is all a matter of choice. I can choose to be anywhere on the continuum.* Again, words can't convey the depth of the experience. I knew when it happened that it was extremely profound. This awakening marked a beginning whereby my heart made a dramatic shift. I'll talk a little bit about this

While talking to my friend Sandy recently, I was telling her of some of the things I had put into this book. At this point I was still writing it. I told her that this knowing that I had the power to choose brought about a knowing that I had chosen this lifetime of physical "illness."

I have come to know that I chose to take on group karma and work it out through my own physical body. I also came to know that I could in any moment choose to have perfect health.

Lester Levenson said that when one reaches a certain state of consciousness one could have
perfect health. He also believed that it is a higher calling to let things unfold without interference. Here is another one of those paradoxes: *To act, or not to act? That is the question.*

Until one reaches a sufficient level of consciousness, one struggles to improve in many ways. Health, prosperity and love are just some of the more common ones. When one reaches a certain point, one loses the desire to change what is in one's own physical sphere. This happened to me after this awakening.

A good example of this is that I used to have to know. *I needed answers* and was on a continual quest to find them. I was never satisfied, and because I had a strong intellect I left no stone unturned. Today most of this hunger has left me and I am much more content.

I also mentioned to Sandy that most people are continually practicing the personality. I said that instead of practicing your personality 24/7 you need to practice the Presence, which is the title of Joel Goldsmith's famous book. To me, practicing the Presence is vital to shift into a place where things naturally unfold and a Knowingness takes over.

While learning from others is a great help, eventually one needs to get it themselves. When one's Higher Self is allowed to waken, one finds that all of the teachings and understandings one has searched for are right there. They are custom tailored to suit the individual, just like a fine suit of clothes.

A point related to this discussion revolves around an interesting statement that St. Paul made. He said, "I die daily." To me this means that he had to let his personality die every day and let his true nature, which is infinite, take charge. A more accurate way to say this might be, "I am continually reborn every moment." If one lives in this manner one lives life with no bias or preconceived ideas. I have taught this in groups that I have taught meditation to.

It greatly helps one enter far deeper meditations. If one enters a still state and just lets every thought, feeling, and moment pass without qualifying it from their own prior experience, then one is truly allowing "living in the present" to take charge. When one lives this way, one is truly free.

At another releasing retreat, I met a participant who told me of *Ho'oponopono*, the art of forgiveness, with ancient Hawaiian origins. I had never heard of it before, though it seemed like everyone else had. I began to experiment with this form of Hawaiian healing and found it transformative. I also found the work of Michael Brown to be very good. Also, I was introduced to the work of Zach Rehder, whom I consider to be one of the best "spiritual" teachers currently out there. His teachings have expanded what was birthed in the Release Technique. It seemed as things were beginning to become much clearer to me. The Universe seemed to be telling me to embrace everything. I started feeling waves of love.

I also changed the manner of my releasing. I had a deep internalized knowing that I was connected to Source. If for example I was feeling concerned or fear, I would say to myself, *Can I let go of feeling fear?* Immediately I would know the distinction between who was feeling the fear and who was not in anything but profound love. I would feel the fear dissolve into the nothingness that it truly is. I should mention here that I believe it to be a healthy practice to feel what one is feeling. As I will discuss in more detail, feeling is one true aspect of meditation.

At my last release retreat, I could see how most participants were merely mouthing statements with little effect. This is what I had been doing before my awakening. I knew I needed to move on.

Chapter 10: Profound Change

By working with love energy, I began to open my heart more. During the previous several years, I had been sending my heart lots of love and healing energy. When I was in my late thirties, I went to a doctor, as I needed a physical to obtain a life insurance policy. He gave me the news that I had something called a "right branch bundle block."

I needed to go to a cardiologist and have more extensive tests done. After a lot of medical rigamorole, I wound up having my regular MD and this specialist perform EKGs. They both showed the same problem: I had a Doppler ultrasound done as a follow-up by the cardiologist. They found no other abnormalities. They explained that my condition might not do me any harm although it did explain why I had had heart fluttering since childhood.

Around 2015, some twenty years after my original diagnosis, I felt something shift in my heart. It had started after my experience with the Release Technique and subsequent work. I noticed myself giving love to whomever I met and to wherever I was. Lester Levinson's "I am you" philosophy became totally ingrained in me. I could more than intellectually know what he meant; I could feel and be what he spoke of.

One day I was at Chicago O'Hare Airport with my son, who was home for college and about to leave to go back to school. His flight was canceled and everyone rushed to get to the counter to get an alternate flight out. In fact, there were many flights canceled and many people at the counter. I was sitting, waiting in line for my son, when I noticed things starting to heat up as they often seem to do at airports.

I started amping up the love I had been sending. Within a couple of minutes the whole atmosphere changed. Everyone was now joking and having a good time. Words cannot describe the change in atmosphere. We left our son at the airport to catch his now re-booked flight, and while driving back home, my wife and daughter commented how nice and loving the airport was under trying conditions. I had never mentioned anything about what I had done and it was another confirmation that I wasn't crazy!

A week or two later, Marla and I were in a restaurant, waiting for a table. The wait was supposed to be a half hour. As we waited in a crowded small space, I had this incredible sense of oneness with all there. Instead of feeling ill at ease, I felt totally comfortable. Again there was a palpable energy of love. I found over the course of the next several months that people would smile at me and want to strike up a conversation with me. Everywhere I went, it was almost laughable how people responded to me. This is the point in which I was initiated past the place of I AM *you* to I AM *that*. I have told people that in my many years as a student of metaphysics my motto has always been "Know Thyself." By constantly trying to dig deeper into my Self, I have had many initiations.

Over the years, people have asked me what I mean by the term *initiation*. I use the term to explain passing a sort of mile marker. It is place whereby one knows they have left the old behind and are entering a new paradigm. Sometimes it can be extremely profound and other times more mild. To me, there is a tangible point where one can still see the past but knows he is headed down a new road.

For the first fifty-plus years of my life I had been met with negativity and abuse. As noted earlier I had a pattern of conflict almost anywhere I would go. Now it was the complete opposite! Murdo MacDonald Bayne's book came back to me. His description of why certain people had that magnetism. I was now experiencing the polar opposite of what I had encountered most of my life. I had made that 180-degree paradigm shift!

As Norm Shealy had once told me, "The purpose of life is to give love." It took tremendous work, but somehow I had shifted into love and it felt great. Somehow I now possessed the ability to change the energy of people and places.

In 2017, I began experiencing some shortness of breath. My doctor, who knew that I had a right branch bundle block, performed an EKG. He told me the scan didn't show any abnormalities. I again went to a cardiologist and he ran a full battery of tests. No right branch bundle blocks or any other abnormalities!

I had a few years earlier intuitively detected that it was gone. I had a profound energetic shift in my heart. The cardiologist told me that the first test must have been bad. He had personally never seen a block of that type disappear. (He did not know I had the test four times by four different doctors and it always showed up.) At any rate, I am convinced it was healed as I opened my heart and found love. A seemingly frightening negative event enabled me to get an extremely important validation. So, again the negative was really a huge blessing!

I believe much of the prevalent heart disease in the world today is a result of people being closed to both giving and receiving love. How many times do you want to say something nice to someone and you don't because of your own fears?

I am now incorporating this love into my healing work. All the things I had learned over the years were being expanded by that love. As I write this in early 2018, Marla and I have decided to sell our beloved farm and move to New Mexico to start the next chapter of our lives.

It is bittersweet to leave a place that we love, where have raised our family. All of the work and love we have poured into this property over the last thirty years is profound. We want a new chapter to be written on this land. We were the stewards of it and now we want someone else to take over and make their own dreams come true. Again, it is difficult to put into words, but I know it's time to leave.

It is interesting to note that during almost three decades of owning my farm, I never thought I would leave it. Then, a few years back, I began to feel that we needed to move. The feeling was surprisingly strong. When I have had similar feelings, they were invariably correct. Marla and I mulled over moving for a couple of years before we finally talked with a realtor. My intuition told me what our farm was worth even though the "comps" were much lower.

I was told by about a dozen intuitives, many of whom I know to be highly accurate, that the property would sell almost immediately, rare for this type of property. During the first year of listing we had no showings! Also, during this time I felt like I was totally clear of any attachments or aversions leaving it. I felt I had really done my homework on this!

We reevaluated the situation and chose a new realtor to represent us, who came to us as the result of another coincidence. Marla and I priced the farm at the lowest price point we would accept. I would not normally price it like this, but we were both perplexed at what was going on and wanted to have a few showings. We were convinced that whoever would set foot on the property would immediately buy it! We had had much interest in the property for years before we thought about listing it, and it is known throughout the county as being a premiere property.

During that first year with the new agent we had nine showings but no one felt about the property like we did. This was strange indeed, as I kept feeling we needed to move, plus intuitives, as well as our own intuition, continued to report to us that a sale was imminent.

I then talked with my friend, Thomas Pecora, and he told me of the sacred nature of the land. He confirmed what I had known for years, that the land was on power ley lines, and that it was sacred Native American land. In fact, he made the additional comment that it had been the burial site of medicine men for many hundreds, if not thousands of years. Thomas had been trained by Wallace Black Elk in many esoteric Native American ways.

Thomas in turn taught me the way in which to properly "smudge" my property and home with sage. I did this, and inside of a month we received an offer. This offer was not acceptable to us, but I do feel it opened up the energy for our potential sale. It seems as if the spirits on our land didn't want us to leave until we found the best possible person to be the caretaker of this incredible property. What strikes me about this whole story is how people can be so insensitive to subtle energies. Also, sometimes the universe wants to play games with us!

Part 2:
Tips to Find Inner Peace

Now that you have a little of my background, I want to share some of my beliefs. I write this section of the book somewhat reluctantly. I say this because of my belief that everything in the present is perfect. I have included the following section as a sort of guide to my own *been there, done that* path of growth. I believe there are many ways to reach a high state of peace and happiness.

I used to believe that one could "screw up" one's life by making mistakes, by not making perfect choices. I now know that everything one does or experiences is indeed perfect. I know many of you will take issue with that statement and say "Yes, but you don't know my circumstances!" Sure, one can take the long way around, and sometimes this road is more painful.

One always receives what one needs to move forward, but I know the Universe gives you the best possible options. It's just that we are too entrenched in our comfort zones to change. A comfort zone sounds good, but it is not always a pleasant place. It can be a place of stagnation and misery, as we are too often simply afraid of change, even if internally we know it is the right thing to do.

Just as with the sale of my farm, there are many reasons why I could choose to hold on. I intuitively know it's time for change even though it's a difficult move. I think many people respond to many different things. Also, where one is, in their spiritual evolution, is very important. To put it simply, one has the power to choose how one feels about his or her evolution and place in the scheme of things. As I stated earlier, I came to a deep understanding that people have the choice to be whoever or whatever they choose to be.

One needs to take responsibility for one's own destiny. Whatever one has in life or thinks he has, can be whatever he wants it to be. This realization comes from a place of profound understanding. It can't be learned from a book. One must read the direction signs one finds along the way.

To get a little complex, I believe that there are parallel universes and phase-shifted realities made up of all possibilities. Also, science is now beginning to see how the universe is made up of a crystalline structure (the Emergence Theory I spoke of earlier). There are also morphic fields that tend to keep things murky due to group consciousness misconceptions. Today's political climate is a good example of this. Everything is on that continuum I spoke of earlier.

Think of your life and one aspect of it. Let's take love for starters. The 180-degree continuum of love is everything from true pure unconditional love to abject hate, or total absence of love. In yourlife, you have probably experienced love or aspects of it in almost everything you have done. If, like me, you had an early childhood experience of love on the low end or hate side, then this determined many of your future life events as they were influenced by this frequency on the love continuum. This is due to the beliefs you formed from these experiences. In parallel lives, there are lives influenced by every frequency of love. Think of all the emotions, beliefs, etc. and you can see that there are virtually infinitely many outcomes, or lives lived.

Don't worry if this doesn't make sense to you as it can only be comprehended by the non-Mind. If you understand it intellectually, then it's a mere shadow of its Truth. I only mention it to you to show that one can change the frequency of anything. ONE HAS THE CHOICE TO BE OR BELIEVE WHATEVER ONE WANTS TO. One needs to take responsibility for oneself.

One common thread I have noticed in my 50-year search for answers is that virtually every spiritual master has said that one has always been perfect. It is not by *the acquiring* that one reaches enlightenment; it is by *the stripping away of illusion*. On this plane most of us think in terms of lack, limitation, and desire.

After my awakening while I was practicing the Release Technique, I found the teachings of Michael Brown and then Zach Rehder. Both these teachers have, in my opinion, similar views. Their teaching reinforced and expanded what had happened when I had my awakening. After much time meditating, it crystallized and is still expanding as I write this book.

In my own words, I believe if you accept what is and know that it is perfect, life starts to unfold in a tremendous way. Again, it's your choice, how you want to experience anything, and how your life unfolds. Resistance, attachment, and desire are the things that stand in our way. One doesn't need techniques to become free, one needs belief that one is free. This statement is another one of those paradoxes! Keep reading and you'll see what I mean.

Anything in one's life is the perfect thing at that time. Let's say that you don't have money. If you choose to know that this is where you are, and you know it's perfect, then you lose any resistance to it and/or you lose any attachment to having lots of money. This is the true "hootless" state (wherein one stops "giving a hoot") that the Sedona Method's founder Lester Levenson talked of. By practicing sending out love to everything one dissolves any resistance. *Where there is no resistance there are no difficulties.* True unconditional Love is the answer.

My healing work has taken a dramatic shift. Mostly what I do now revolving around healing is working on a much larger scale. I am not so much engaged doing individual work as I am in doing world or regional work. Whether it be on a large scale or individual, I now see things as whole and perfect. All I need do is visualize the perfection. If my doing this accomplishes change (letting go of illusion) then, great! If it doesn't (on the relative level), I still see perfection.

I can go on and on, but this is the simplest way to achieve a high state of Being. If you ask the *hows* and *whys*, see if you *are* in your mind. The answer, if you are truthful, is YES. This can only be experienced, not understood intellectually, although I say fake it until you make it.

CHOOSE to know that no matter what, you are getting what you need. If you are getting what you need, why be upset? Just send out waves of love to everything in your life! One must not practice this method to *cause* change, as then one is not in the true hootless state. If one is truly okay with where one is, then one doesn't desire change. Once in the hootless state, all you need to do is state your preference: "I am poor, but I'd prefer to have enough money to do whatever I want to do, whenever I want to do it."

I was recently told, "I am sick and the doctor tells me I need to do so and so."

I replied, "If it seems prudent to do so and so, then do it. It's your responsibility to take action, or not." I told him, "Do what you feel you need to do, but be okay with not only being sick but by being confused about the whole thing. Open yourself up and feel all those feelings and don't judge them. Know that you have the power to change it all, but do what you need to do in the present moment."

There is a paradox here (and seemingly everywhere), where one can cannot comprehend with the rational mind. One may ask, "Why even try and achieve a 'higher state?' If what you are saying is true, then you should be okay with where you are!" There is some truth in this, especially for people who are spiritual seekers. Like me, most seekers are really trying to improve. I needed to let go of that trying and yet follow my inner guidance which has driven me to find answers to life's deepest mysteries. This is where one's personality needs to fade away with all of its desire for improvement in one's life experience.

Meditation is a big help. This is the other common thread in all the teachers I know who have reached enlightenment. Meditation can be many different things. Don't think of it in terms that limit it.

Meditation is a state of being. Meditation can be experienced while one is in the true "feeling" realm. It can be experienced by simply being aware of the breath, or countless other ways.

As an aside, I should explain what I mean by the term "enlightenment." I believe there is an infinite continuum of consciousness. Just like my description of the 180 degrees. Hence there is an infinite continuum of enlightenment states. Where does one want to consider the point of enlightenment on the continuum? Is it 180 degrees or 75?

The Sufis say there is an upward spiral of Consciousness. When one reaches the top or Unity with the One then one starts the downward spiral and back up again if one wants. I mark the (arbitrary) point of enlightenment as the point where one feels true continual contentment and peace. Also, at this point I believe the questioning mind loses its dominance and Presence takes over. Again, it's a place where one knows when they reach it.

I believe that what I have just said in the previous few paragraphs is enough to push anyone to a highly advanced state, a state in which there are few or possibly no more attachments, no more resistance to anything. It is a state of true peace. Here one finds one doesn't need to *do* anything, just *be*.

I believe many additional techniques are beneficial. Some of these include working with the energy field, *chakra* work (recognizing the centers of spiritual power in your physical body), and color therapy, which includes working with the rays.

Other beneficial modalities to raise consciousness are archetypal work or working with the archetypal energies, and/or angels, past life work, and creative endeavors including all types of artistic endeavors.

None of these however, is as good as simply choosing to be what you want to be. This choice is fundamentally as simple as choosing to be okay with what is. I can't say it enough!

I also believe that one needs to be aware of where one is in every moment, physically, mentally, spiritually, and emotionally. Take stock of this many times during the day. Feel how energy shifts. See how you shift. See how your environment changes continually.

One's perception becomes increasingly more sensitive as one practices this. Again, this could be the subject of another book. This is the truest way that I know of to be continually and completely in the present moment.

Some specific ways which I think will help to expand one's consciousness:

Remember what I said earlier, that there is really no expansion, only a stripping away of illusion.

The following are presented in no order of preference. The first is writing from the soul. The second is past life work. The third is listening to uplifting music and crystal frequencies. The fourth is getting into the feeling realm and seeing what comes up in the body/energy field. The fifth is color therapy. The sixth is crystal work.

All these modalities I have personally done, and also facilitated them in a workshop setting, with positive results. Again, it is easy to get sidetracked into these modalities. Remember to, at least daily, check in to see what you want to change in your life. If you want to change it, you don't think it serves you!

Remember, everything you currently have right now is PERFECT! If one assumes that everything is perfect and asks the question "Why is this perfect?" will lead to great insight. e.g., *Why is having no money perfect for me? What good comes from it? How does it serve me?* This list is not the only thing one can do, and they are not in any specific order. Try them out and see if you resonate with them, and if it helps you to come to a place of peace and acceptance of what *is*.

Writing from the Soul

I found that I have the ability to "channel" words from what is, for me, my Higher Self. After doing this personally for many years I tried it out in a workshop setting many times with total novices. I have found that 'most everyone is able to gain profound insight from this type of work. Not only does one gain basic insight from this practice, but also one begins to open up a strong connection with one's soul. One starts to discern the "still small voice."

Whether people channel from their subconscious, higher selves, or guides, they receive insights that can free them from many limitations. The only people in whom I have seen this method fail are those who suffer from what I previously called Spiritual Elitism. They simply refuse to believe either that this could be possible or that it will help them.

A good prerequisite is meditation although one doesn't have to be familiar with meditation to benefit from it. My instructions would be to simply find a quiet spot and focus on your breathing. If you have a special spot in nature, you can go there either physically or in your imagination. Cultivating your imagination can also be a great practice.

If you practice imagination, then be as specific and detailed as possible in your imagining. Once there, focus on your breath. You don't need to breathe in a specific way although one can pursue breathwork courses if one desires. There are many good teachers out there. One that I am familiar with is Dan Brule's courses or workshops. Also, Zach Rehder is very big on breathwork.

Focus on your breath for about five minutes. Have a notebook and pen readily accessible at your spot. After approximately five minutes, you should be more centered. If not, don't worry; just keep practicing, keep your attention on your breathing.

Now start to write whatever comes to you. Something will. Once you start, do not stop writing, even if it reads like gibberish. Pausing kills the flow and lets the mind in. Keep writing, even if you think it is coming from your mind. Pick a time limit for your session and have an alarm sound when that limit is up. Three to five minutes is a good starting point.

Once you stop, don't read what you have written for a while. I usually wait a full day to read it. Do not throw out what you have written, even if it doesn't make sense. Practice this for several weeks. You should feel like it is getting easier to do. Save what you write; never throw it out!

I have found that keeping a folder or journal with all your writings of this sort is beneficial, even years after you have written them. Play with this and I believe you will find some great insight into your inner nature and what you need to help you attain a happier life. In any event, this endeavor helps to open and helps you to recognize your Inner Voice more easily. It really puts one in the present moment.

What I have given here is a basic way to get started with this type of practice. Again, play with it and make it your own. You will find that you have written some profound things that in many cases only you can appreciate.

Past Life Therapy
Find a good coach, psychic, or practitioner who specializes in past life work to begin to find what unresolved issues are impacting your current life. I have used many different people for this, along with doing a lot of this work on my own. Luckily, I found out that I have the ability to trace many energetic

patterns back to their roots. For me, this speeds up the process of past life therapy immensely. Norm Shealy offers courses at Holos occasionally to become certified in this type of work.

One of my most memorable experiences with past life work was inspired by a simple exercise. During one of my Parker workshops years ago, he led the group on a guided meditation, where he had his etheric music playing low in the background. With his great, soothing voice he led us into a deep meditative space. He then "guided" us into a room where we saw a large armoire. He told us to open it and we saw several sets of clothing.

He said to pick out the first set and put it on. For me, I saw what my intuition/mind's eye said was a Roman centurion's uniform. I put it on and was guided to go into that lifetime. I readily experienced being in a tent or structure with several of my commanders. They told me I needed to take my men into battle. I protested as I knew we would all be killed, but the order stood: "Yes, but it's for the good of Rome." I knew I had to follow orders.

I remember feeling sad, not for me, but for my men, whom I knew would be uselessly killed.

I saw myself in battle the next day and remembered the slaughter. At one point I was fighting an enemy soldier and had taken him down to the ground with my sword at his throat. He appealed to me for his life. I stopped and thought for a moment, *Oh well*, and just ran him through with my sword. This behavior is not something that I would think of doing in this life, but in that life it was what I was trained to do. The vision soon ended and I went on to experience two other different lives, vividly.

As a side note, during my quest for information on the Putnam life, years after my meditation experience, several psychics told me of a lifetime as a Roman soldier that was still having an impact on this current lifetime. One went into a rather detailed account which helped me heal. She described a similar, almost identical scenario as my meditation.

After the battle she saw all the dead lying on the battlefield. She saw my soul rise out of my body and hover over the carnage. She revealed to me my soul's reaction to what had transpired. *What a waste! I was responsible for all this death. My loyal men trusted me and I led them into a slaughter.*

I felt tremendous guilt in not fighting my superiors, even if it meant my own death.

I felt a big energetic release and let go of a lot of responsibility and guilt as a result of the psychic's story.

Sound Therapy/ Crystal Frequencies
This is the modality that I have used the most to help me over the rough spots. While everyone has different tastes in music, each of us needs to become aware of how the music or sound affects our body/mind.

At first, experiment and find music that puts you in a calm tranquil state. Generally, I find that New Age or Meditational music is the best for this, though other types can work well to clear blocks and "move" energy. For me, New Age works the best to put me in a meditative state. I use this when I write most of my channeled material. I often use "guided meditation" while listening. I often guide myself with preplanned "ideas." Oftentimes they may turn out totally unexpected and I can follow them through straightforwardly. I should mention that using sound/music to meditate is not always ideal.

Spend time in silent meditation. In these times one may hear the Celestial Music. Kriya masters caution to not get enthralled by this as it can be a huge distraction to moving deeper into Consciousness. I have also used crystal bowls. I really like these to clear out blocks. Many people experience memories related to issues they should work on, while listening to these sounds. There are many different frequencies and types/sizes of these bowls. If you can, go to a shop specializing in these and try some out. There are some websites that offer samples of the sounds, though I prefer to hear them in person. In workshop settings I find most people are moved by the sounds of these bowls. It seems to be a favorite of my class participants.

Also useful are the Selfaggio Frequencies available on line. These sounds have specific frequencies for various issues or areas of the body/bodies. Gregorian Chants have a similar effect. Still, I prefer New Age music and crystal bowls for most of my work.

Enter Your Feeling Realm
Everything is energy. True feeling is out of the mind and into the Self. This is the purpose of meditation. Stripping away of the learned reality and feeling the Real.

My apprenticeship with Larry lasted several years. During the whole first year all I did was go into the energy of various plants. The first one was a Norfolk Pine I had in my meditation room. In essence, what I was doing was to feel the plant. This then developed into truly being able to feel my own body. This was foreign to me as I had learned to suppress my feelings and was afraid to feel due to my childhood. Eventually things opened up and I learned to move into the energies of others (with their permission).

One of my first experiences after my year of plant analysis was moving into a computer that I was repairing. This was one of the most fascinating experiences of my "reading energy." Words can't convey what I felt/experienced. Suffice it to say the energy/consciousness of that computer was fascinating. I felt a strong connection to all people that had ever been "through" that computer. What I mean to say more specifically is I felt all people who had ever been on line. Now I build all of my own computers, as I became fascinated with their energy.

For most readers, I would say to sit in a meditative state and systematically go through your physical body. Start with your feet and feel what they feel like. Spend at least five minutes with just your feet.

This is a lot of time for most people. If your attention wanders, simply bring it back. As you practice and you get more comfortable with this, move on to the calves, thighs, pelvis, stomach, chest, throat, and head.

I suggest you start with the physical body until you feel you can comfortably move into any part of your body and "read" it. You will fairly quickly develop the ability to read your whole body in a few minutes. Then you can move on to the chakras, and/or other energy bodies if you desire. Reading the book, Focusing, by Gendlin is another recommendation I have related to this.

This technique assists greatly in becoming adept at meditation, healing of the physical body, as well as assisting in clearing/healing the energy bodies. There are many practitioners that can guide you into this type of work.

An important point regarding feeling is what I mentioned earlier. Due to its importance I will repeat: *when you feel, allow all of your conditioned learning to drop away.* Feel as if you had never felt before; there will be no judgment. How would you feel if you had just been born? Again, this allows Presence to take charge!

Light Therapy/Crystal Work
We all have subtle energy bodies and chakras. There are many books about this. One book

that I especially like is Barbara Brennan's book, <u>Hands of Light</u>. There are many practitioners who read peoples' subtle energy. Some practitioners specialize in chakras, others in one's subtle bodies. There is much information on these topics available.

One exercise that I often use relating to color therapy is to intuit what color frequency or "ray" I need to work with. I then call in that color and visualize being bathed in that color. Again, I am doing this in an altered or meditative state. I will at times feel a particular angel come in and sometimes look up to see what angel is associated with that particular color. I will call in that angel and ask for assistance.

I have long been attracted to color and particularly to the concept of rays. As stated elsewhere in this book, I feel that I intuit many things that most other intuitives don't receive. I notice this especially in my healing work.

One thing related to rays that is somewhat different from what I have heard from others: I believe there are sixteen rays, or colors, that pertain to our galaxy. I believe a dozen of these can be used by humanity currently. The other four will be able to be accessed, but later. I also believe that there are another sixteen rays emitted from the center of the Universe.

These observations do not matter much in terms of working with them. I simply mention this to put it out for other healers or intuitives to look into.

A simple guided meditation that you can do when learning about this work is to visualize going into a large circular temple. Inside this temple, directly in the center, is a large chair or throne. Sit down and you will see that you are sitting in the center of a spoked wheel. Each one of these spokes has a different color; seven of them are the corresponding colors of the chakras. You may also see other colors or combinations of colors associated with some of the spokes.

Pick one color that you feel drawn to, get out of your chair and move down that colored spoke (pathway) until you come to a door which is that particular color. Open the door and go inside.

In the center of the room is a large comfortable chair or throne. Sit down and you notice your guide standing beside you. You may ask for any information or help you may need. Inside this room you are bathed in your chosen color. It permeates your entire being, clearing, cleaning and clarifying. Stay as long as you like. When it's time to leave, get up and move out of the room and out of the temple. Then gradually come back to the present.

Imagination is sometimes much more transformative than our perceived 3D reality! Many books are available on the meanings of color and how they may relate to chakras. If in doubt about meanings, ask. Answers can be found.

Again, with any guided meditation one can find a practitioner or friend to lead you or you may want to do it yourself. Many people will script a meditation and record it with their own voice. You can even dub your preferred music using many programs available. As my intuitive abilities started to gel, I found I had the ability to communicate with crystals. I was drawn to specific crystals. I have many crystals in my meditation room and feel bathed by their energies. I was pleased when visiting Norm Shealy one day, when I walked in on him and an electrical engineer.

Norm was giggling like a little kid and holding a large quartz crystal in his hand. He was connecting it to a Tesla coil. He put it down and told the engineer to turn on the juice.

Norm was as excited as a kid getting an ice cream cone! He later explained to me that he was experimenting with charging crystals. Norm uses various crystals extensively in various projects and apparati.

I would recommend picking out several crystals that you are drawn to and try and meditate with them. While you are in a quiet meditative state, see if they want to convey any ideas or messages of import to you.

There are many books on the subject which you should, if you feel drawn to them, by all means read. If you desire healing of a particular chakra, you can get a crystal associated with that chakra and put in, on, or near that chakra with the intent of having a healing.

There are several techniques on "clearing" the energy of crystals. The one I usually use is to simply put it in the sun for a day or two with the intent of having the crystal cleared of any "lower" or negative energy. One can imprint crystals with various instructions or healing energy. This could be the subject of another book. Again, if you are drawn to crystals play with them! Many healers use them in their work.

Epilogue

In summary, the preceding techniques are simply things that I have enjoyed and I also feel have helped my journey. I have given elementary starters for these, which may help some of you. As mentioned, you don't need to do anything. It is my hope that this book may inspire you to move forward in your journey with joy and love.

My life may have turned out totally differently had I not encountered metaphysics. Had I not remembered and re-remembered many of my experiences, who knows what may have happened?

The Universe does not act out of malice, whim, or luck. You will always get exactly what you need to move forward!
Take responsibility for what is in your world! If you don't like it, change it! Only you have the power to do so; just remember: There is a Purpose in everything that happens!

###

About the Author

Dean Andrea was born in Chicago in December, 1956. After suffering years of bullying and abuse he went on a lifelong quest to find answers to some of life's most perplexing questions.

Mr. Andrea is an accomplished golfer, businessman, and family man while being a hidden metaphysician.

His fifty-year search included becoming an energy healer of body, mind, and spirit as well as deeply delving in to past lives of his own and clients. He also spent years studying many abstract teachings until he finally found the deep peace and freedom most people long for.

Pre-publication Comments

Dr. Norm Shealy:
Many Americans suffer ridicule, abandonment, and abuse in childhood. Few of them recover and live even a reasonably happy life. Rarest of all is the unique one who thrives and develops a successful spiritual action model.
Here is that exception!

Cheryl Murphy, psychic medium:
Dean Andrea's book is a biographical tale of perseverance through terrible emotional damage until he was finally able to arrive at a self discovery of love and belonging in his mind and spirit.
Reading about his quest was an inspirational and meaningful experience for me.

To you, dear Reader:
Thank you for reading my book.
If you enjoyed it, won't you please take a moment to leave me a review at your favorite retailer?

If you are interested learning more about Dean Andrea, please connect to his website at: www.abridgetothesoulbook.com

Dean Andrea -- A Bridge to the Soul

www.ingramcontent.com/pod-product-compliance
Lightning Source LLC
Chambersburg PA
CBHW030441300426
44112CB00009B/1111